To Tom
I hope you ...
book #3
Malawi! John Wood
May 11, 2014

Acknowledgements

I would like to thank my husband, Captain John Wood, who made our dream of cruising to the Rio Dulce a reality. I thank my mother, Pat Guthrie, who I will always think of as my biggest fan. I thank John's parents, Ann and Bill Wood, for instilling a love of travel in their son and for their unending support of our lifestyle. I thank our children - Sylvia, Suzanne, Samantha, Donna and Donald, for their love and support.

Thanks to Lori Soule for the many hours she spent proofreading. Thank you to Donna Lay and Rick Davidson for proofreading for me. I thank Lisa Brewster for her help selling books back in Canada while I am away in paradise. I thank my many supporters - in Canada, Roatan, and elsewhere.

"Adventure is a path. Real adventure – self-determined, self-motivated often risky – forces you to have firsthand encounters with the world. The world the way it is, not the way you imagine it. Your body will collide with the earth and you will bear witness. In this way you will be compelled to grapple with the limitless kindness and bottomless cruelty of humankind – and perhaps realize that you yourself are capable of both. This will change you. Nothing will ever again be black-and-white." – Mark Jenkins

ISBN 1481888994, 978-1481888998

Cover and book design by Melanie Wood
Editing by Lori Soule
Illustrations by Melanie Wood
Photos by Melanie and John Wood
Printed in the United States

Published by Diamond Lil Publications
Oak Ridge, Roatan, Honduras
504-9870-4477
johnmelw@hotmail.com

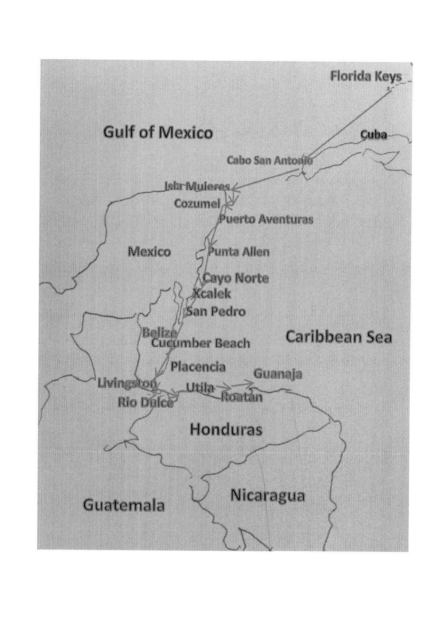

Chapter 1

Florida Keys

June 12, 2007

A sense of déjà vu washes over me as I film the vessels in the mooring field of Boot Key Harbor. They're lined up like sardines in a can, all pointing neatly in the same direction.

Boot Key Harbor, Marathon, in the middle of the Florida Keys, has been home for the past ten days. Our previous three visits to this popular port of call have been during the winter months and we are overwhelmed by the heat and humidity of summer. We dive immediately into our shower each time we return from a trip to shore. The harbor is eerily quiet, with few boats equipped with generators and I feel a little guilty as we run ours each evening so we can enjoy a little air conditioning.

There are also few outboard motors on the dinghies in the harbor and most of the locals row in and out to the dinghy dock. It is a very different place than the busy, tourist-filled town of winter. The locals refer to this as "a nice time of year, before it gets too hot." It makes me glad we're leaving. Then again, we're heading south.

We fly the only Canadian flag in Boot Key Harbor; a grim reminder that hurricane season is on its way. The stores are full of tax exempt items that the locals stock up on as part of their hurricane preparedness and we took advantage of these sales.

We're off on our next great adventure, a cruise to Guatemala's exotic Rio Dulce. In order to provide coverage for hurricane season, our Canadian insurance company offered us three choices. We could spend the season north of the Hudson River, the option we chose last year when we returned on *Diamond Lil* to Canada for the summer. We could travel south as far as Trinidad or we could travel up the Rio Dulce in Guatemala.

The trip to Canada from the Florida Keys and back is about 4,400 miles. Last year, in 2006, the cost of the diesel fuel we used to make this trip was $8,000.00. Then there was the cost of marinas and meals along the way. We had already traveled up and down the Atlantic ICW and down the inland rivers and were looking for a new adventure. The trip south to Trinidad, although appealing, requires open water passages beyond *Diamond Lil's* capabilities and fuel range.

John had dreamed of traveling to the Rio Dulce after reading several articles about the area. In 2006, we asked our insurance broker if she would insure us for the Rio Dulce, but she had not been able to offer this as an option for the 2006 hurricane season.

One year later, after receiving similar inquiries from other customers for coverage in this increasingly popular area, our broker offered to present our request to the underwriter and asked us to provide her with more detailed information to assist with her presentation.

We provided website addresses of marinas in the Rio Dulce region, which included information about the distance from the Caribbean Sea, marina security, and assurances that we would stay with our boat at the marina for the duration of our stay. We were thrilled when our broker reported back to us that we would be granted coverage to travel to the Rio Dulce for the 2007 hurricane season.

Hurricane season begins officially on June 1st, but with our trip home to Canada in May, there was no possible way for us to be in the Rio by this date. Knowing that hurricanes at the very beginning of the season are rare, our insurance company granted us an extension. We have until July 1st to arrive in the Rio and have *Diamond Lil* secured in a marina slip. Once there, we must fax back proof that we are docked at a marina with an armed security guard, in order for our insurance to be valid. For this coverage, we have been billed a Caribbean surcharge.

Our basic insurance rate, from July 1, 2006 to June 30, 2007 is $1,489.00. This provides us with $130,000.00 coverage on *Diamond Lil*, $3,500.00 worth of coverage for our dinghy and outboard and $5,000.00 worth of coverage for our personal effects.

To travel to Florida costs us an extra $750.00 for insurance. The Bahamas surcharge is $300.00 and above that our Caribbean surcharge is another $400.00. That is a total of $3,089.00 per year. OUCH!

The heat is not the only thing overwhelming me as we prepare for this daunting voyage, for as much as we have researched our destination; we are still heading into the great unknown.

We have been cruising on *Diamond Lil* for two years
now. In 2005-2006, we completed the Great Circle Loop,
a series of lakes, rivers, canals, and waterways that
connects a huge area of south central Canada and the
eastern United States. I wrote my first book, Diamond
Lil Does the Loop, about this trip.

We spent the winters of 2005 and 2006 cruising around
many of the Bahamas Islands. My second book,
Diamond Lil Does the Bahamas, was born of this life-
changing experience.

We have plenty of space on the boat, including an extra
cabin for visitors, a large, nicely laid out galley, and a
roomy and comfortable back deck for enjoying the
outdoors and fishing. Also, our fly bridge allowed for
increased visibility when "reading the water" in the
Bahamas. And with wraparound windows in the cabin,
we enjoy a 360-degree view of our surroundings.

However, there is no "perfect" boat, and the very
characteristics that made for great cruising around the
loop and in the Bahamas presented us with a new set of
challenges as we planned our trip from the Florida Keys
to the Rio Dulce.

Our shallow draft and high fly bridge, a godsend in the
past, would become a handicap as we traveled across
the Gulf of Mexico and down the Caribbean Sea to the
Bay of Honduras. The prevailing easterly winds we
would encounter as we hugged the eastern shore of the
Yucatan Peninsula and northern Belize would result in
uncomfortable beam seas. Without sails and without a
deep keel to steady us, we anticipated a rocky ride.

The refrigerator and freezer are stuffed after another
Marathon provisioning trip. Our first stop was the giant
Wal-Mart in Florida City on our way down to the Keys,

not a pleasant task, but a necessary evil. Opting to keep
the rental car that we had picked up at the airport for
an extra day, we took advantage of our temporary
wheels to load up at the Kmart, Winn Dixie and Publix
stores in Marathon.

Despite having the car for a day, the provisioning went
on for many days and frequent trips were made along
Highway A1A. An odd pair we were, the captain on foot
and me riding alongside on my bicycle. Nursing a case
of plantar fasciitis, more commonly known as boater's
heel, I am attempting to stay off my feet as much as
possible, not an easy task when living a mostly
pedestrian life.

Taking advantage of the hurricane sale at Home Depot,
we purchased ten extra five-gallon gas cans, requiring
two trips to the dreaded hardware giant. John loves to
browse endlessly up and down aisles of tools and
gadgets, boring me to death. If possible I wait outside,
foolishly believing that he'll be faster if he thinks I'm
waiting in the hot sun.

John carried back four cans on his first trip, which he
made solo, much to my relief, and four on his second
trip, with me pedaling alongside on my bike carrying
the two extra cans strapped around my shoulders.
Pedaling slowly enough to try to stay with a pedestrian
is not easy and I'm sure the traffic passing by figured
me for someone who had spent a few hours at the
Overseas Bar.

Our greatest challenge on this trip will be our limited
fuel capacity. We carry 300 gallons of fuel, enough to
travel approximately 500 miles, with no currents

factored in. The distance from our jumping-off point in Florida's Dry Tortugas to Islas Mujeres, just off the eastern coast of Mexico, is 292 nautical miles.

However, with no fuel available for sale in the Dry Tortugas, we must fuel up in Key West, a total of 333 nautical miles to Isla Mujeres. Factoring in the clockwise flow of warm water through the Yucatan Straits, known as the "Gulf Loop Current," averaging approximately two knots, but at times as much as five or six knots, we realized that we would be cutting it close.

One option was to stop in Cuba to refuel. However, our insurance company would not cover us in Cuban waters and we had heard horror stories about boats checking in and out of Cuba. We were on a tight schedule, in order to reach the Rio by July 1st, so we wouldn't be able to spend much time in Cuba.

"We'll plan to go straight to Isla Mujeres," said John, "but we will be prepared to stop in Cuba if we need to." We had bought a Cuban courtesy flag, charts and cruising guides, in case we needed to stop there.

Considering another fuel option, John priced a flexible diesel fuel holding tank, which would ride on deck, at $560.00 US. In the end, we opted for the five-gallon gas cans at the hurricane sale for $5.00 each. This would provide us with 50 extra gallons of fuel, a comfortable buffer, at a savings of $500.00 over the fuel bladder option. Besides, I didn't relish the thought of a stinky fuel tank riding on the bow. That's where I ride!

Every nook and cranny in the boat is packed tight. The double bed in the guest cabin is stacked high with supplies; enough to last us for the next several months. John has been busy getting the boat ready for our long trip. He changed the oil filters on both engines and the generator and both fuel filters, a job that requires the flexibility of an acrobat. We hauled the old, black oil into the marina by dinghy to dispose of it.

We hired two divers to clean the bottom of the boat for $100.00. The good news is that we'll recover that easily in fuel savings. The bad news is the divers have reminded us that we need to replace our anode. So, once again, we walked to the dreaded Home Depot, this time to buy a new drill bit to make the holes in the new anode plate, or zinc.

A sacrificial anode is a relatively inexpensive piece of metal (approximately $100.00) which is bolted into electrical contact with other, more expensive metal components. Zinc anodes extend the life of the boat's hull, engines, rudders, propeller shafts, engine cooling systems, refrigeration condenser and other metal components by protecting them from deterioration caused by galvanic corrosion. It isn't nearly as much of an issue in fresh water but the salt water had corroded our anode so that only about a quarter of it was left. We first noticed it in the Bahamas but couldn't find the part there, so we had to wait until we returned to Florida to replace it.

The anode plate is attached under the water line which makes it extra tricky. John had to measure what was left of the old one to buy the correct size, measure the bolt holes on the old one, or what was left of it, and place the holes on the new plate in the correct position. Once drilled, there was a little modification required on one of the three holes, which he made with our handy Dremel tool. There were a few tense moments for me, as he disappeared under the water to attach the zinc. It's heavy and I dreaded the possibility of him losing it under water, but the job went smoothly.

With the zinc replaced, hubby dove into the next job. This one had him lying flat on his belly on the galley floor, reaching bodily down into the bilge to attach the new shower discharge hose, because the old one was clogging up. My job was to stand quietly by and pass tools, flashlights, and cold drinks.

Our second major challenge, before we set out, is to overcome the anchor-dragging issues we experienced over the winter, riding out the constant northeasters blowing through Georgetown, Exumas.

I have always preferred anchoring to staying at a marina, but several hair-raising episodes left me less than enthusiastic about swinging on the hook. With our shallow draft and a large, high area for the wind to push on, we would swing violently when the wind changed direction. This often results in us dragging our anchor.

The night that we ended up sitting sideways on the beach in front of the Chat and Chill Restaurant on Stocking Island was the last straw. Admittedly, it had been an unusually windy winter in the Bahamas, and ours was certainly not the only boat to drag anchor during these episodes.

But we knew we would need to upgrade our ground tackle if we were ever to sleep soundly at anchor again. The trip to the Rio Dulce would require spending many nights at anchor, some of them in fairly open, unprotected spots. We decided to upgrade our main anchor, a 50-lb. CQR, to a 66-lb. Bruce, leaving the 35-lb. Bruce as our secondary anchor and two Deltas for additional backup. We sold the 50-lb. CQR anchor.

The black pirate flag that has been flying on *Diamond Lil's* bow for the past couple of months is tattered and torn, and I've never liked it. I blamed it for bringing us bad luck, for when we flew it in Georgetown we were swept into our nightmarish series of anchor dragging episodes.

Therefore I am happy as we head down highway A1A once again by bus, to Key West. We are shopping for our big, new, bad-ass anchor. We also need new anchor line, for our spare anchor, to replace the one that was severed during one of our hair-raising squall experiences in Georgetown this past winter. Much to my relief, we are also headed to our favorite little Key West flag store, to buy a new bow flag.

The bus ride to and from Key West can be almost as entertaining as the town itself. It isn't at all like a bus ride back home in Canada, where people get on, sit in silence, and then get off. Most of the seats face towards each other on these Keys buses. People get on and introduce themselves, if they don't already know each other, which most of them do. Often the conversation continues for the entire hour and ten minutes of the ride.

Sometimes you pay to ride the bus and sometimes you don't. Yesterday on the way down we asked for a day pass and the driver didn't have any, so we rode free of charge. On the way home the driver asked before leaving Key West where everyone was going. She remembered and stopped along the way at each place, not necessarily a designated bus stop, but wherever the passengers wanted off.

On this day, we are entertained on the bus ride by Bicycle Joanie. The first thing I noticed about this odd, little woman was the two white plastic bags that she was wearing over her shoes. They were tied around her beanpole-thin ankles. Shiny pantyhose clung to her skinny legs.

Up the stairs she climbed, greeting the driver and then all the passengers, including us. I wanted desperately to ask about the bags, but couldn't get up the nerve. Luckily for me, one Keys character could not resist asking.

"I'm on my way to work," said Bicycle Joanie. "This is the only pair of shoes I have left. All the rest were ruined in Hurricane Wilma. So, I have to keep them clean for work."

I found out later from our good friends, Joe and Wendy, who had spent time in the Florida Keys, that her nickname was Bicycle Joanie. They told me that she had run for town council last year. She had not been successful, but that didn't keep her from participating in the politics of her Keys.

Politically active to the extreme, she called a member of town council as we rode the bus, passing her cell phone to each passenger in turn, including John and me, so that we could voice our opinion on a particular bus stop that she wanted changed to a more convenient location. Talk about a direct line to your member of council.

Our shopping trip was a great success. We came away with a new Conch Republic Flag for the front of *Diamond Lil*, enjoyed lunch at one of my favorite eateries on Duval, walked the streets and stopped for a cold brew. We finally climbed aboard *Diamond Lil* around 11:30 pm, way past our usual bed time.

The next morning, while I logged the damage from our shopping expedition to Key West, the captain made a final trip to Home Depot, for grinding disks. He needs these to grind down the end of the new anchor, so our swivel will fit into it.

The provisioning is almost done. We are waiting for two new batteries, as well as fuel and oil filters to be delivered, so that we have a spare set on board for the next change.

While changing the oil in the generator, John noticed that the zinc anode on it needed to be replaced also, so that was done. We're getting close.

June 13
12:00 pm

Leaning out my fly bridge window, I filmed the mooring
field slip past, as we bid farewell to Boot Key Harbor. I
have always longed to make the trip to Key West on
Diamond Lil, and finally, it's happening. Following
Hawk Channel, which runs along the south side of the
Keys, we enjoyed a pleasant, 51-mile trip to Key West,
under sunny skies.

As we rounded the western tip of Key West and veered
east, bright afternoon sun cast a bright red glow on the
Custom House Museum, just behind Mallory Square.
As the anchorage came into sight, we were as surprised
at the contrast between late spring and winter here, in
Key West, as we had been in Marathon.

We've made the trip down A1A many times during our
winter visits to the Keys, always by bus, but never on
Diamond Lil. The marinas are expensive and the wide
open anchorages are unprotected from the nasty
nor'easters that roll through, making life aboard
miserable. We had seen very few boats anchored offshore here during our winter visits. We were shocked to
count 200 boats within sight from where we anchored,
with perhaps an equal number out of sight, in another
part of the mooring field.

Slap, slap, slap - is the sound the waves make against
our hull, as we lounge in our blue canvas boat chairs on
the aft deck, taking in our new surroundings. A cruise
ship shares the seawall with a Coast Guard cutter.
Power boats whizz through the harbor and a float plane,

with a giant phone number painted in bright red on its wings, buzzes overhead. Sailing vessels are clustered around Wisteria Island, more commonly known as Christmas Tree Island. It's a busy place!

For the first time, we can enjoy the Key West nightlife without rushing to catch the last bus back to Marathon, which departs around 10:00 pm. We savor a delicious buffet dinner on the open air patio at Captain Mario's, entertained by the streams of colorful passers-by. Sneaking up a flight of stairs to an empty room, I found what I was looking for - a bird's eye view of Duval Street.

We meandered down to join the throngs of tourists at Mallory Square, who were toasting the sunset and pursuing the elusive green flash. Then, the streets were ours to wander. With no nasty curfew to dampen our spirits, off we went for our last night of decadent American revelry.

June 15

With butterflies in my stomach, I watched as John filled the diesel tank on one side of *Diamond Lil*, and then the other, and finally the ten bright red, five-gallon jugs that he had lined up on the aft deck. This was it - all the fuel that we had to make it to Mexico.

The first leg - 74 miles - from Key West to the Dry Tortugas National Park, with its famous Fort Jefferson, is on the agenda for today. We'll spend the night anchored there. Hopefully, weather permitting, we will set off for Mexico tomorrow morning.

The Dry Tortugas is considered part of the Florida Keys. This little group of islands to the west of the Keys was originally named Las Tortugas (the turtles) by explorer Juan Ponce de Leon, in 1513. The word "dry" was later added to warn mariners of the lack of fresh water available there.

The reefs surrounding the Tortugas helped to form one of the most strategic harbors in U.S. history. Fort Jefferson is located on one of the seven Dry Tortugas Islands. It was one of the largest forts ever built, taking 30 years (1846-1875) to complete. During the Civil War, the Tortugas were used by Union warships to blockade southern shipping and as a prison, mainly for Union deserters.

The most famous prisoner held at Fort Jefferson was Dr. Samuel Mudd, the physician who set the broken leg of John Wilkes Booth. Mudd was convicted for allegedly participating in a conspiracy to assassinate President Lincoln and sentenced to life imprisonment, but was later pardoned by President Andrew Johnson in 1890 and freed from the fort.

6:15 pm

The Tortugas are home to Loggerhead, Green and Leatherback turtles. They swim bravely around *Diamond Lil* in our scenic anchorage here and I'm trying desperately trying to catch them on film, but they're too quick.

I feel like we've stepped into the horror movie "The Birds". The skies are black with thousands of screeching, squawking birds. The park is home to 299 species, some that nest here and others that migrate in the spring and fall. Some of the most common species are the Sooty Tern, the Magnificent Frigate bird, the Masked Booby, the Brown Noddy, the Ruddy Turnstone and the Brown Pelican. Both the sight and the sound of thousands of birds, hovering over and nesting on a tiny island, are amazing.

The Tortugas is known for its wonderful snorkeling, so with *Diamond Lil* safely settled, we pulled on our swim suits and plunged into the clear, turquoise water. The people from the power boat anchored in front of us were jumping into the water, scrambling quickly out, and laughing hysterically. Noticing the puzzled looks on our faces, they pointed over at the water by our boat.

A Goliath grouper, also known as a Jewfish, the size of a Volkswagen, swam just inches from our feet. It was every man for himself as John and I scrambled over top of each other, grasping for the ladder, to climb to the safety of our swim platform.

We had read about the giant fish that lived here at the park and had planned to do some snorkeling. But as I watched schools of enormous fish leaping from the water in an effort to get away from the even larger fish, I decided that I was cool enough already. I amused myself by feeding hotdogs to the monster Jewfish, baiting him to get him close enough so I could take his picture.

I snapped a shot of the captain, perched on the side of *Diamond Lil*, wearing only his brown and beige paisley swimming trunks and a navy ball cap with the word Canada on the front.

The late day sun cast a reddish glow on his tanned skin as he stroked his beard and stared off to the west, deep in thought.

The sky above small, low-lying Bush Cay was thick with hundreds of thousands of birds. A huge sign read ISLAND CLOSED. We learned that it was nesting season, and so the island was closed to protect the birds.

"I know we can't land there," I said to the captain, "but let's take the dinghy in close so I can get some footage of this, before we head over to the fort."

We edged up as close as we dared. The entire island was covered in them - every branch of every tree and the top of every reed. The sky over our heads was thick with the squawking birds. It was as if they were chasing us away and away we went, off to tour the fort.

From a distance, the fort appeared to take up the entire area of Garden Cay, the small island it was built on. A broad moat surrounded four of the six walls. The other two walls were built to the sea's edge. The red brick hexagon was three tiers high, surrounded by openings which at one time housed 410 heavy guns. The largest masonry structure in the Western Hemisphere, the fort was built with over 16 million bricks.

It was from here that we would set off tomorrow morning, on our longest crossing to date. Plan A was to head for Isles Mujeres, just off Cancun, Mexico. Plan B, should plan A fail, due to bad weather and/or excessive fuel consumption, was to head for Cuba.

Originally, plan B (Cuba) was the plan of choice. So, when we flew back to Canada, we purchased a Cuban courtesy flag, Cuban charts and a Cuba cruising guide. However, once we read the cruising guide and learned more about the complex and expensive system of paperwork required for clearing in, moving about from port to port, and clearing out of the country, we preferred the Mexico option.

Our barbeque, perched on the transom, sizzles away with smoky treats as the sun kisses the horizon and then slips away. Tomorrow, when it peeks back up, we'll be on our way.

June 16

Early this morning, my frustrated captain attempted to get a weather report from the kind folks at Fort Jefferson.

"We can report on the weather to the east of us sir, but I'm afraid we cannot report on the weather to the west," the gentleman who answered the radio told John. A few, ungentlemanly words escaped hubby's lips, as I lunged for the hand held radio just in time to prevent him from being prosecuted for uttering foul language on the VHF radio.

Anticipation overwhelmed us as we set off early this morning on the next leg of our great adventure. Despair is more the emotion that we felt a short while later, as we limped back from our first attempt to set out from the Dry Tortugas. Fourteen miles is all that I scribble into my log, a mere fraction of what I had anticipated.

We aborted our plan after only seven miles, when we cleared the reef and found the seas too rough to continue. Flashbacks of trips we had made in the past, and wished we hadn't, entered my mind.

The captain was of the same mind as he turned the ship around, retraced our route, and re-anchored by Fort Jefferson. All we had accomplished was a wasteful depletion of our precious fuel.

Doubts and misgivings about this trip into the great unknown blew this minor setback out of proportion. I sulked and stewed and then when night fell and we crawled into bed, I snapped at the captain and charged off with my pillow under my arm to sleep in the guest cabin.

The guest cabin has no hatch over the bed, like our cabin does. I only punished myself, as I tossed and turned in the sticky June heat, while the captain stretched out and enjoyed the entire bunk in our breezy, cool cabin.

June 17

A sense of déjà vu filled the cabin this morning, as we went through the same motions as yesterday morning, receiving the same lack of cooperation in our attempt to get a weather report from either the Coast Guard or the park rangers.

With fair weather, we can cruise straight to Mexico. This will take us about 49 hours, or two days and two nights. The plan looked favorable until about 3:00 pm, when the wind picked up sufficiently to render the seas quite nasty. My light lunch of two pieces of jerk chicken became fish food as I became suddenly and violently seasick. Overwhelmed by heat, I tried everything I could think of to cool off.

John gave me some Dramamine and put a cold cloth on my neck as I laid on our bed, with a fan plugged into the inverter blowing straight on me. The waves bounced me around and I found no relief. I climbed into the tub, ran a few inches of cold water and sat, sloshing around, holding the shower door as it crashed and banged back and forth. Unfortunately, relief eluded me. I had taken the Dramamine too late and I retched, over and over. I tried to lie on the floor of the aft deck. It felt cold against my skin. John ran up and down from the fly bridge, dividing his time between emptying my bucket, nursing me, and driving the boat.

"Try to sit up long enough to watch over the side. I have to go up and secure our secondary anchor," he said to me, as I lay heaving on the aft deck. I knew he was serious when I saw him put on his life jacket. We buried the anchor pulpit as *Diamond Lil* crashed into each wave. I could barely hold myself up long enough to keep an eye on him and started to panic at the thought of him being swept overboard.

I watched in horror as John climbed along the slippery side decks, and then dropped flat and worked his way to the bow on this stomach. I stood watching him, helpless to render any assistance, as he fought with the crashing anchor and finally re-secured it with duct tape. What would we do without it?

"Please, please, can we stop in Cuba?" I begged him. "I can't take this."

"Yes. Ok. I have already changed course," he agreed. "I have to keep the revs up with this bad weather. We're using too much fuel. Better to stop in Cuba and re-fuel."

His words brought instant comfort and I found a spot on the settee, in the cabin, where I could rest and hold on to our large captain's table, keeping both it and me from tossing about. I had visions of us pulling into a nice Cuban marina and enjoying a sound sleep, tied to shore.

The hours dragged by as I lay in agony. Darkness fell and still we kept on moving. Finally, I mustered up enough strength to climb up to the fly bridge.

"Why don't I see land, yet? I thought we were going to stop in Cuba," I asked the captain.

"We are," he said. "We are heading for Cabo San Antonio on the western tip of Cuba. We'll be there about two o'clock tomorrow afternoon."

"What! You must be kidding." I wailed. "You mean we have to drive through this all night?"

"I'm afraid so," said the captain. "Are you feeling any better? Do you think you could take over while I go and get some rest? I'll probably drive most of the night, so I'd better get some rest now, while I can."

I did actually feel a little better by this point, so once I got over the shock of discovering we had another day to endure before we reached Cuba, I put on a brave face and took over the helm. With little choice but to keep the bow turned into the waves, we followed the coastline of Cuba all that night and the following day.

We maintained a minimum distance of 12 miles from shore, as suggested by our Cuba cruising guide, and even then we were shadowed by a couple of vessels, no doubt the Cuban coast guard monitoring our movements. It was slightly unnerving, but the light of day eased conditions a little.

With the dawn came the heat. I could not bear to have my arms touch my sides as I tried to read my book, and I could feel the heat of each breath as I exhaled. I propped pillows around myself, trying to create a little shade from the sun. Then I propped up my book, *The Perfect Storm*, to try to block the sun. The hours stretched on and on, as I followed our course to the west, wondering if I had made a good choice of reading material for my time up here alone at the helm.

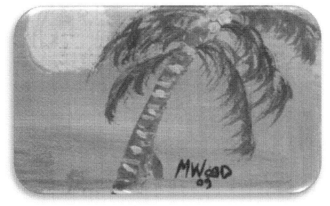

The mooring field in Boot Key Harbor, Florida Keys

We hired two divers to clean *Diamond Lil's* bottom

A sailboat we passed as we traveled along the Hawk Channel

The view as we pulled into Key West

The ten extra jerry cans we bought in Marathon

Filling up with diesel fuel in Key West

The famous Whistle Bar on Duval Street in Key West

Our favorite place to buy boat flags – in Key West

Approaching Fort Jefferson in the Dry Tortugas

Captain John, cooking our dinner in the Dry Tortugas

26

Fort Jefferson – Dry Tortugas

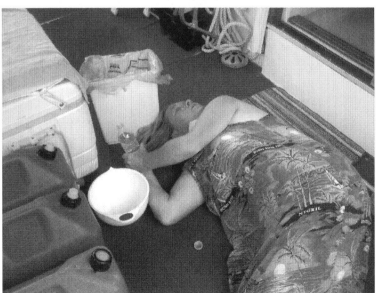

Admiral Mel – feeling seasick on the way to Cuba

Chapter 2

Cuba

June 17, 2007

We were within sight of Cuban land when the heat overcame John. He downed a bottle of cold water, which came right back up. So, all of a sudden I was at the helm, bringing *Diamond Lil* through the channel towards Marina Gaviota at Cabo San Antonio.

Downstairs, John leaned over the side, taking his own turn feeding the fish. I called on the radio, in English, out of habit, and of course received no reply. The Spanish phrases that I had practiced were lost as my mind went blank.

"*Hola. Hola,*" I heard, followed by a rapid succession of instructions, none of which I understood. Two men waved their arms about and pointed at the spot where they wanted us to dock *Diamond Lil*.

We did as we were told, hopped off, tied up, and were greeted once again with "*Hola,*" by the dockhands, who turned out to be two of the endless series of officials we were soon to meet. We stepped off *Diamond Lil* and set foot, for the first time, on Cuban soil.

Quickly flipping through my notes, I managed a weak, "*Quiere una bebida*?" John flipped open the lid of our cooler and displayed a variety of soft drinks, beer, and water, spread out on an inviting bed of ice.

"*Si, una cervesa, por favor,*" said the first man, and John tossed him a cold beer. His face lit up, as he popped open the top, took a long pull, and passed the can to his buddy.

"It's ok. Here - have another one," John said, tossing them a second can of beer. They thanked us profusely as they wandered away, chattering between themselves, in Spanish.

A few minutes later, we saw them heading our way again. This time they were pushing a large plastic garbage can on wheels towards the boat. The can turned out to be full of diesel fuel. They filled the generator and started it - just for us. We were all alone; the only vessel at the marina, which seemed just a tad creepy.

The procedure for clearing into Cuba is lengthy, complex, and carried out by mostly Spanish speaking officials. The procedure is to enter flying the yellow quarantine flag with the Cuban courtesy flag above it, but because John was too sick to attach the flags to our 27 foot-high aerial, we got by with just the Q flag on our bowsprit.

The immigration officer strolled down the cement dock and greeted us. He informed us that *La Guarda* must clear us in before him, apologizing for the wait, but insisting that procedure must be followed. *La Guarda*, however, is not here, so we must wait *treinta* (30) minutes, for him to arrive.

I pulled out the *Spanish for Cruisers* book we had purchased at the Nautical Mind bookstore in Toronto, along with a Spanish/English dictionary, and we chatted - half in English, half in Spanish, with the odd French word thrown in - while we waited.

Eventually, the immigration officer learned that the *Guarda* on duty was out fishing and unaware of our arrival. His partner, a lovely woman named Tatiana, arrived. She apologized about her lack of uniform, in fluent English, and explained that she was not on duty. However, since the *Guarda* was out fishing, she would fill in for him.

She asked us several questions about last port of call, our plans for cruising Cuba, our next port of call, the length of our stay, and our home port, and explained that the doctor was on her way.

Tatiana interpreted for the doctor, who spoke no English. We were asked about our health and assured her that we were both healthy. I wondered, as I did so, which of us looked a more ghastly shade of green.

She made sure we had no pets on board, made a brief inspection of all rooms in the boat and filled out the first of many forms. Once this was done we were able to remove our quarantine flag.

We could not leave the marina until we obtained visas, she told us. Because it was Sunday evening and worse yet, Father's Day, the other officials were not at the marina.

We watched the news (in Spanish) with Tatiana, who was the warmest, friendliest woman you could ever hope to meet, interpreting for me. We had already decided to stay and rest for at least a day, more if the weather didn't calm down.

We fell into bed, too hot and exhausted to eat, thankful for the power to run our a/c and feeling pretty smug. Despite the horrors we had heard of, we had only had two lovely ladies on board and so far hadn't spent a dime.

June18

The illusion of a simple and inexpensive check- in to Cuba lasted only until this morning.

I was sitting in my comfy deck chair out on the dock savoring my very first Cuban sunrise along with a delicious cup of hot coffee in my favorite black china mug.

My reverie was shattered when, at 6:30 am, the officials began to arrive. The immigration officer took our passports. Yes - he took them away. At first I thought he was going to keep them to make sure we didn't leave until we were cleared out but eventually he returned with them in hand. With him came three more officials; the customs officer and two different ministers of agriculture.

We offered them water, pop (soda), or beer. Two of them accepted soda and the others chose beer. It was 6:30 in the morning. Two of the four spoke fairly fluent English. The two agriculture ministers spoke none and we carried on a comical question and answer routine in Spanish and English, with a little bit of charade type activity on my part.

One fellow checked all the meat, milk and eggs in our refrigerator and freezer, making notes on all of them including where they were purchased. He couldn't read English so I answered his questions with pig snorts, chicken gestures and moo sounds. That got a few laughs from all of them, including John.

We had to show them all our prescription and non-prescription drugs (Tylenol etc.) and once again they listed them all on another form. They left us with our copy of many forms and wherever we go we must carry them all, along with our visas and our passports.

The entry costs and regulations regarding the conversion from American dollars to pesos were explained to us and it was surprising to learn that each charge was multiplied by 1.2368. The charges were $35.00, $25.00, and $14.00 with the added 1.2368.

Then we had to go up to the marina office to pay for our visas - another $30.00 or $37.11. The price on the fuel pump said $3.90/gallon and John put in 100 gallons, expecting to pay $390.00 - but no, it came to $482.35.

Yikes! And they do not take credit cards, so thank goodness he brought lots of cash. We still had to pay for the slip which at 40 cents a foot x 38 feet = $15.20 x 1.2368 = $18.79 per night. Then, there is an exit fee of $10.00 or $12.369 pesos.

"I don't understand, John." Why are we converting dollars to pesos and adding this surcharge to everything if we are still paying in dollars?"

John just shook his head. "I don't really get it either. But we are in Cuba so we just have to pay it, I guess."

John was getting pretty upset by the time we paid for the fuel and we were almost out of cash. Luckily there are no stores anywhere near here, so we don't need the cash but we wanted to have some on hand when we arrived in Mexico.

We were told that three kilometers away there was a hotel where we could use our Visa card to get cash. We set off on our boat bikes, as soon as the officials all left, eager to explore Cuba.

We almost died of sunstroke. No, we were told, we could not get cash there. We would have to go another 61 kilometers to the nearest bank. Since the three kilometers had almost killed us, this was out of the question.

We were so hot that I stripped down to bathing suit top and a pair of unattractive underwear and went in for a swim at a gorgeous but deserted beach. Just like our marina, the hotel was empty. And, like the marina, it was just a bit creepy.

Upon return to the boat, we both showered and flaked out like a couple of wet blankets. We thought we were done with officials, but all of a sudden another one came along the dock with the immigration minister and a dog - to search for arms and drugs. We knew of course that we had neither on board but it was still an intimidating experience.

I snapped photos of the officials completing their paperwork and this thrilled them. They were honored that I wanted to take their picture. We passed out more beer and gave Wanda, the search dog, some water.

The dog owner spotted a can of WD-40 sitting on the counter and said something in Spanish to the immigration minister. He interpreted for us that the dog owner could really use some WD-40 for some rusty bolts in his home. This, he told us, they could not get here.

John reached down into the cupboard below, and found another, full can, so he tossed the partially full can to him. You would have thought we gave him a hundred dollar bill. He was so tickled with his can of WD-40.

We had read about the lack of availability of most items in Cuba, so when I walked up to use the washroom in the marina, I did as instructed in our cruising guide, and took a small roll of toilet tissue with me. The roll was almost empty, so I left it there.

"Did you see the doctor and the other woman?" asked John, after I walked the long, cement dock, back to the boat.

"What do you mean?" I asked.

"After you left the washroom, they came out with your roll of toilet paper. They split it and took half each.

There couldn't have been more than four sheets left on it," he told me.

We took the ladies each a big, fluffy, new roll of tissue. We also took a bag of decadent American cookies to the office, for the staff to share.

I had seen what one man had brought for lunch when I was in the office earlier. He had only two small white buns with a bit of butter. That's all.

On my printer in the boat, I printed the photos I had taken of Tatiana and some of the staff and gave them each a copy. They were giddy with excitement over the photos.

Hopefully the weather is calm and we can be on our way to Isla Mujeres in the morning, after an exit inspection of the boat to make sure we are not harboring any Cubans. Other than the officials, it is against the law to invite any Cubans on to the boat. Our one day in Cuba cost us large but we are safe, sound and well rested.

Marina Gaviota at Cabo San Antonio, Cuba

The Cuban officials, filling out a lot of paperwork

Diamond Lil, taking on diesel fuel from a barrel in the little shack

Diamond Lil was the only boat at the marina in Cabo San Antonio

Wanda, the Cuban search dog, with her handler

We added one of our old flags to this collection at the marina

Tatiana, posing for a photograph at the marina

Chapter 3

Mexico

Isla Mujeres
June 19, 2007

After the long, agonizing trip to Cuba, the next leg of our journey, to Isla Mujeres, Mexico was a piece of cake. We were up at the crack of dawn, anxious to set out at first light, in order to reach our destination before dark. No such luck. It was 9:15 am before we were cleared out of Cuba.

First, though, we had another serious Cuban official visit the boat. He filled out several more forms and searched the boat one last time, for anyone we might be attempting to smuggle out of the country.

An enormous following sea hastened our 135-mile trip. After 13 pleasant hours, shapes began to take form as we neared the island. We had read about the wonderful anchorages here but we certainly weren't going to attempt to anchor in the dark. The mismatched white pilings on a long dock glowed in the dark.

As we edged up to the dock, the shadows in the dark became a cluster of fishermen. With a great deal of enthusiasm, they waved their arms in the air and shouted out orders, in Spanish.

"They're pointing over there," I said to John. "I think they want us to put her on the inside of the basin."

"With the wind and the current, I'm not going to attempt to back *Diamond Lil* into the spot between those boats in the dark. If they really want us to, we can move in the morning. Besides, they don't look like they work here. They're just fishermen," insisted the captain.

We pulled in along the outside wall, sending the fishermen scurrying out of our way as we tied *Diamond Lil* to the broad dock.

"Come on. Let's check it out," said the boss, after we closed up the fly bridge and put away our books and guides.

"The guides all say that we can't leave the boat until we check in," I pleaded.

"You worry too much. Don't be silly. The streets are full of tourists. Who is to know?" said hubby.

Off we went, breaking the rules again. Of course, he was right. We blended in with all the tourists, out for a stroll on a balmy Mexican evening. The streets were alive with music. I filmed a group of teenagers as they entertained the crowds with lively tunes on their steel drums.

June 20

Tied to the dock here in Isla Mujeres, I felt a huge sense of relief. The worst was behind us. The trip from the Dry Tortugas to Cuba had been rough. Yesterday's jaunt, from Cabo San Antonio to Isla Mujeres, was much easier, but still a long travel day. We slept like babies, knowing we were tied safely to shore.

Before 9:00 am, the dock master was at the boat with the first of more forms for us to fill out. He arranged to have all the officials come to us for a small fee, which we found out was well worth it after speaking to other cruisers who ran around contacting the officials themselves.

Once again we had the food in our fridge, freezer, and pantry inspected. It was a breeze after the experience in Cuba, and by about 10:00 a.m. our quarantine flag was down and we were free to explore the island.

Isla Mujeres was discovered on March 4, 1517 by Francisco Hernandez de Cordoba, who led an expedition from Cuba. He named the island Isla Mujeres, meaning Island of Women, because of the numerous terra-cotta female idols he found at the Mayan temples and shrines. It is believed that they were dedicated to Ixchel, the Mayan goddess of the moon, fertility, and childbirth.

By mid-morning, the tourists began arriving from Cancun. Boatload after boatload of them poured out onto the dock, crowded the beach and filled the narrow little streets of town. Late afternoon brought the return of the massive ferries. Quickly filling to capacity with tourists, off they would zoom to the fancy hotels in Cancun.

Then the island takes on a quieter, more peaceful feeling. There are still tourists in the hotels but they are few in number compared to the multitudes that arrive from Cancun.

At around 8:00 pm tonight, John and I went out for a walk. We were amazed to find that only a few hours after the hordes had left, there was not a single piece of garbage on the broad white beach, nor in the narrow, little streets. Neatly tied garbage bags lined the *Malecon*, ready for pick up the following day. It is a refreshing change, after the litter we saw almost everywhere in the Bahamas.

Strolling back along the *Malecon*, we discover an inviting beachside restaurant. Bright red plastic Coca Cola tables are shaded with bright yellow Sol umbrellas. Weary from hours of walking, we cannot resist stopping for a cold drink. I savor a frosty margarita as I kick off my flip-flops and dig my toes into the warm, snow-white sand.

The place is decorated with huge murals of brightly colored fish. John rolled his eyes as I made the rounds, collecting fish photos. I have been painting pictures of fish since we arrived in the Bahamas, and I'm always eager for new ideas.

For our last dinner in Isla Mujeres, John savored coconut shrimp the size of chicken legs and I chose seared tuna coated in sesame seeds with ginger, soya and cilantro. My taste buds have died and gone to heaven.

June 21

"It's a shame that we're on such a tight schedule," I whined to John, as we enjoyed our coffee this morning.

"I just love it here. I know we planned to leave this morning, but we really should do our laundry first."

Our Canadian insurance company has granted us a one month extension to reach the Rio. Theoretically, hurricane season begins on June 1st. However, hurricanes are very rare this early in the season. In order for our insurance to remain valid, we must be there by July 1st.

"I know what you mean," said John. "One more day won't hurt. We can go tomorrow, if you'd rather."

We stuffed our dirty laundry into our handy, extra-large, heavy-duty Ziploc dry bags. We loaded them onto our little cart on wheels, pulling it along the bumpy cobblestone road to the *lavanderia*, where the sign claims that they are wash experts and do not mix loads.

"*Cuanto tiempo?*" I asked the wee woman behind the counter.

"*Tres horas - a la una,*" she answered and I was thrilled that I understood.

"What did she say?" asked John, as he followed me out on to the street.

"Three hours. At one o'clock." I told him.

Anxious to pop my first postcards from Mexico into the mail, I dragged the captain along a series of narrow roadways, to the post office. Fourteen more pictures from paradise were dropped into the mail.

Next stop was Adrian's Internet Café. I surfed in air-conditioned luxury, surrounded by people speaking Spanish. I do believe that I am actually beginning to understand them.

Periodically I reach into my purse, where I keep a little notebook of handy Spanish phrases.

Solo estoy mirando - I am only looking. This is very useful when we are browsing through the souvenir markets.

Puedo la cuenta por favor - Can I have the cheque please?

Cuanta cuesta - How much does it cost?

Cuanto tiempo - How long?

Somos de Canada - We are from Canada

Ok, I know it's not much, but the list is growing longer each day.

June 22

Leaving Isla Mujeres, we headed towards Cancun, six nautical miles across Bahia Mujeres. After we crossed the bay, we followed the coastline for several miles, heading west. I panned slowly along the shoreline, catching mile after mile of snow white sand lining the shore.

Hotels, too numerous to count, lined the beach. Set back in the sand were hundreds of them. This is where all those enormous ferries brought the tourists from every day, I thought to myself. No wonder Islas Mujeres had been overrun with them. I panned along the continuous line of hotels from Punta Cancun to Punta Nizuc with my video camera. I am very glad that we were heading for Cozumel and not Cancun.

Satisfied with having seen the place from the water that until now I had only seen on the glossy pages of travel brochures, we headed offshore into deeper waters and made course for Isla Cozumel, another 45 nautical miles to the south.

Cozumel is Mexico's largest Caribbean Island. What a rush it is, to finally be in the Caribbean Sea on *Diamond Lil.* A swift four to five-knot current, running against us, made for a long trip. It took us over eight hours to cover only 51 miles.

However, it was a perfect day on the water, with a light breeze and only a few, puffy white clouds in the sky. There is nothing like a little fishing to pass the time on such a glorious day. Russ and Suzanne presented us new fishing tackle when we visited Canada last month. They wanted to thank us for the great day of mahi-mahi fishing we enjoyed in the Bahamas.

It took no time at all for one of the colorful new lures to work its magic. I rushed for my video camera as John strapped on his fishing belt and got to work bringing in the fish. I captured our bright red and white Canadian flag, flapping gently in the wind. I filmed the thick, white fishing pole, bending under the weight of the fish.

John tossed off his ball cap as he struggled to reel in his prize. He had on beige shorts and a short-sleeved, cotton shirt, white with a beige paisley pattern. He reeled and pulled, reeled and pulled, over and over; grimacing with the pain in his poor, arthritic hands.

I held my focus on the spot where I expected the fish to burst from the water. Surely this time, I would catch it, before he yelled at me to put down the camera and get the net. Through my lens, the waves, as we wallowed in the sea, were making me seasick. They seemed much bigger now that we had slowed down.

Finally tiring of filming the churning sea, I gave up and readied the net. We were rewarded for our effort with a beautiful skipjack tuna, also known as Oceanic Bonito or Striped Tuna.

Late evening sun peeking through heavy, dark clouds lit up the fronts of the low-rise buildings along the shore, as we entered the Cozumel harbor. I filmed a Disney cruise ship that was leaving port and heading to sea. The sea was a blinding silver color, as the sun caught the surface, forcing me to turn away.

I was shocked at how few boats were in the harbor. There was only one cruising boat anchored - a catamaran. A pirate-type tour boat passed us heading in the opposite direction in the otherwise empty bay. I guessed that they were tourists, heading out on a sunset tour. An enormous green, red and white Mexican flag waved above shoreline.

We dropped anchor about 200 feet from *Avenida Rafael Melgar*, also known as *Malecon*, which is the street that runs along the waterfront.

"I want to go for my first swim in the Caribbean Sea," I said to John, as I pulled on my bathing suit.

"Well you better go quickly, because it's getting dark and I need to clean our fish. I can't do that while you're in swimming," he said

I popped in for a quick dip. I floated for a minute, looking up. Then I looked down and it was deep and blue and clear and there, right under the boat, was a huge barracuda, watching me.

"Oh man, I hate them. Why do they always find me?" I moaned, racing for the ladder.

I snapped a few shots of John, cleaning the fish, bare-chested and wearing his denim ball cap. On his left hand, he wears a fish glove, so he won't cut it off with the razor-sharp fish knife that he holds in his right hand.

A fine end to a fine day, I thought to myself, as we watched the sun set over the Caribbean Sea and feasted on fresh tuna.

June 24

The island of Cozumel is 28 miles long by 9 miles wide
and was discovered in 1518 by Juan de Grijalva, from
Cuba. The name comes from the Mayan word "Ah-
Cuzamil-Petén" which translates to "Land of the
Swallows". We are anchored just off San Miguel, the
only city on the island, where all the action is.

We can see Playa del Carmen across the water,
approximately ten miles to the west. Large, fast turbo-
driven ferries fly back and forth between here and there
continuously, carrying both passengers and vehicles.

Cruise ships make port here and spill thousands of
passengers onto the streets for the day. Vendors in the
busy downtown area welcome us and attempt to
separate us from our *deniros*. At first they cannot
distinguish us from the *touristas*, the ones who spend
muchos deniros.

We have no room for souvenirs on the boat and politely
explain this in our English-Spanish lingo, "*el barco*, no
walls, no places" I tell the woman who is trying to sell
me her beautiful paintings. "*Solo estoy mirando* - I am
only looking."

The people are clever. Before long, they recognize us on
the street and remember us. We are not buying and
they know it.

We pass the trendy, touristy restaurants along the main
drag and walk back into the town, where the people of

this city of 50,000 live and eat. Here there are few *touristas* and we find a little *loncheria* where the food is less than half the price and more traditional. There is less English spoken here, so we are forced to use our Spanish. I point to a woman's meal at the table next to us.

"*Polzone*," the waitress says. *Polzone* it is for me. *Polzone rojo pollo*, actually - red chicken something. It's a soup and it's delicious served with corn chips and lots of lime.

The *Museo* (or museum) provided refuge for us from the hot afternoon sun, along with plenty of historical information about the island. There were numerous Mayan artifacts on display.

Afterwards we found a shady spot in the Plaza del Sol to sit and rest our weary feet for a while; then hobbled back to the boat, where I had a long siesta.

Sunset found us back on shore, for an evening stroll up and down the *Malecon* and around the Plaza del Sol, where dancers and musicians performed. We experienced our first Mexican rap music act.

June 25

Our first stop on the Yucatan Peninsula will be at Puerto Aventuras. Our two Mexican ports-of-call have both been on islands. The captain wants to fill up the

fuel tanks and has found a marina with diesel fuel for
sale.

Looking forward to a short, 18-mile trip, I am perched in
my usual spot up on the fly bridge. As usual, we have
our cruising guides and charts upstairs with us.

"John, have you read this?" I ask, as I get to the part
about entering through the cut to the marina we are
headed for.

"Yes, I read it. That's why we've been waiting for this
weather. You can only enter under perfect conditions,"
he answered.

Despite the fact that my trustworthy captain has
prepared himself, I read aloud from our guide.

*"A flashing red light marks the rocky shoreline at Punta
Fatima. A flashing green light and two green buoys
mark the channel to port. You'll enter through this
narrow channel on a course of 357 degrees.*

*This pass can be extremely dangerous when the trade
winds kick up sizeable waves onto the reef awash and
the rocky shoreline. Entrance depth is 8.5 feet. Several
boats have broached ending up high and dry on the reef
or rock jetty. I would not attempt this pass in raging
conditions. When you make your approach be sure to
come in with enough engine speed to maintain full
control of your boat. The marina offers a courtesy escort
service to guide you through this sometimes harrowing
pass. They stand by on channel 16 or 79, 24 hours a*

*day. If you have any doubt, take them up on this
service."*

"That sounds scary, honey," I moaned. "Maybe we
should call for an escort."

"Don't be silly," he laughed at me. "There are no rage
conditions. I told you I checked the weather. We're
fine. We have two diesel engines. They are referring to
sailboats, that can't get enough power to control the
boat. You worry too much."

"Ah. John! You didn't tell me the slips at this marina
are med-style. You know I hate when we have to back
into a slip like that. I always have such a hard time
with the lines," I wailed, as I read on in our cruising
guide.

"You'll do fine. You worry too much," repeated John.

Puerto Aventuras Marina is about half-way between
Playa del Carmen and Akumal, in the middle of the
Mayan Riviera. The marina is only a small part of a
much larger, 900-acre, world-class residential
community and golf resort. There are five-star hotels,
condos, private beach villas, and houses to choose from.

Despite my fear of med-mooring, I am excited as I read
on in our guide. There are many restaurants, lots of
shopping, and the very popular swim-with-the-dolphins
attraction.

As we neared our destination, I filmed the long stretch
of buildings lining the shore on each side of the cut.

Matching yellow walls glowed in the afternoon sun
under matching terra-cotta roofs. Set back behind
stretches of white sand, on and on they went, tucked in
behind brick walls, their private yards dotted with little
grass *palapas.*

Before long, we were steaming at a good clip up the
middle of the rocky channel, which was as described,
quite narrow. Even with the calm weather, the surf
crashing on the rocks not far from our starboard side
and on the beach to our port side was intimidating.

My dread of mooring med-style was postponed as we
pulled directly into the fuel dock. I felt a sense of relief
as I stepped off onto the high cement wall and tied
Diamond Lil to the cleats.

We topped up our tanks with diesel fuel, at a cost of
$211.00 and forked out $55.00 for a slip for the night.
For another $120.00 U.S., we could swim with the
dolphins.

Instead, we wandered through the amazing complex,
browsed through the touristy shops, and stopped for a
delicious meal.

I satisfied myself with videotaping the flocks of tourists
swimming with the dolphins. The dolphins were
trained to do some amazing tricks, but the loud and
raucous display wasn't at all what I imagined swimming
with one of the peaceful creatures would be like.

A volunteer from the group of swimmers was told where
and how to stand in the pool.

"Go, go, go, go!" the dolphin trainer shouted, encouraging the crowd to chant along with him.

On cue with the chanting, one of the dolphins swam up under the volunteer, invisible in the water, until the moment the swimmer was scooped on its back for a quick trip down the pool. The crowds clapped and cheered.

Another woman was shown how to hold on to a dolphin's fin and ride on its back along the length of the pool.

A young girl on a flutter board was held in position by a trainer.

"Go, go, go, go, go, go!" chanted the crowd, on and on, as yet another dolphin pushed the child on the board, down the length of the pool.

Tiring of the incessant cheering, clapping, and chanting, we wandered away from the noisy display and found two dolphins, quietly minding their own business. I zoomed in close for some amazing footage of one of the dolphins, as he looked at me for the longest time.

Finally, he let a loud gush of air escape his blow-hole, dove under the surface of the water, and swam away.

After exploring the massive resort, I started to wonder what the area was like outside the complex. We had come in by sea, so I had no idea what the land was like.

"Let's go out past the gates for a walk and see what it's like out there." I suggested.

"Sure," said John. We worked our way out, along a very well-manicured entry and past the guards who manned the massive orange cement entranceway.

The moment we stepped outside the resort, we were in another world. As we crossed a bridge that led over a highway, we looked down on a military roadblock. Army vehicles were sideways on the roadway, blocking a long line of traffic. Army personnel lined the roadway. One was sitting in a military jeep, his head poking through a hole in the roof, manning the roof-top machine-gun.

On the other side of the bridge, we found a small village, known as the Puerto Aventuras Pueblo. This, we had heard, is where most of the employees at the resort live. The narrow, dirt roads were flooded with water from a recent downpour.

It looked like some construction was underway, creating quite a mess. Despite the water-soaked streets, people were going about their business. Most of the homes were one-story cement structures with rough openings cut for windows and doors. Rebar poles poked up through most roofs, as if there was more building to be done, later.

We stopped at a little *tienda* and bought a couple of soft drinks. I practiced my Spanish, for there was no English spoken here.

"Do you feel nervous?" I asked John, as we were the only non-locals on the street.

"No, not particularly," he answered. "But I wouldn't want to be here after dark."

As much as I hated to admit it, neither would I.

June 26

Mother Nature foiled my Plan A for today. We had hoped to stop at Tulum to visit the most spectacular Mayan Ruins on the east coast of the Yucatan. It was only about 30 miles from Puerto Aventuras.

It is a day time anchorage only. Knowing this, we planned to stop for a few hours, explore the ruins, and then continue on to La Bahia de la Ascencion to anchor for the night. It was heartbreaking to only see the impressive *El Castillo* from the water.

"Hopefully we can stop and see it on the way back," said John.

He made the right call about skipping Tulum. It was a rocky 62-mile ride to Punta Allen. As I filmed him creep up to the bow of the boat, to secure an anchor that had bounced loose, I wasn't too sure about a return trip on *Diamond Lil.*

"You must be joking," I whined as we lurched about for hours on end. I really hope we like Guatemala because there is NO WAY I am ever making the trip back, at least not on this boat."

We spent a lazy night anchored at Punta Allen, a small remote fishing village at the north end of the Bahia de la Ascencion. It is a large, shallow bay, considered one of the best lobstering grounds in Mexico. It is popular with sport fishermen because of the bonefish and permit found in the shallow water and also provides great refuge for cruisers heading north or south along the Yucatan coast.

June 27

Another long day brought us 80 miles further south, to Cayo Norte on the Chinchorro Bank. At one point, I braved the rocky trip down the ladder and through the boat, looking for a new book to read along the way.

"John, come quickly," I shouted, dashing back up the ladder to the helm.

"There's something terribly wrong. I think we're taking on water. The master stateroom floor is covered in water and so is your side of the wall," I wailed.

"Here, take over," said John, leaping out of his captain's chair.

Visions of us sinking out here, never to be seen again, flashed through my mind as I waited for John to investigate. The moments dragged by as I waited for the verdict.

"It's OK," he finally called up, as he climbed up the ladder to the fly bridge.

"Our wash-down pump sprung a leak. That's all. The water all came in while you were pulling up the anchor at Punta Allen, but we had no way of knowing until you went down for your book. We are not going to sink."

Relief washed over me as I took in the news.

"I soaked up most of the water from the floor with as many towels as I could find. I can't do anything about the pump until we stop. You'll just have to do without it," said hubby.

"Oh, man," I moaned. "The anchor is always coated with slime when I pull it up. So are the first few feet of chain. The boat is going to be a mucky mess without the pump."

"A minute ago you thought we were sinking. Now you're worried about a little mud. Relax. It's not a big deal," said John.

I have been looking forward to this anchorage since we read about it in our cruising guides. The Chinchorro bank is one of only four true atolls in this hemisphere, with the other three found in Belize.

An atoll is a kidney-shaped platform reef; 26 miles long and 6 ½ to 9 ½ miles wide. An atoll is a coral ring, rising perpendicularly from great depths, enclosing a central deep basin lagoon. The little spot in the middle of the ocean brought to mind the old television show Gilligan's Island.

In order to protect the reef, the Mexican government formed the Chinchorro Bank Biosphere Reserve in 1996. There is no fishing, conching, or shell-collecting permitted. I had planned to do some snorkeling, but a huge, hungry-looking barracuda, lingering just under our swim platform, changed my mind.

It was very odd to be anchored in shallow water in the middle of the deep ocean and John sat up half the night on anchor watch. Our big, new anchor held beautifully but it was a bit unsettling way out there. Enough atolls for me!

We had some visitors while we were out in the middle of nowhere. Six members of the Mexican Navy tied up alongside and four of the men boarded us. They were actually very polite and friendly. Five of the six men were actually just kids, but they still carried M-14s. The older fellow searched the boat quickly and became really friendly when he saw pictures of our kids, asking all about them, in Spanish of course. It wouldn't be Mexico if they didn't fill out more paperwork and demand to inspect the paperwork from our previous port-of-call.

June 28

The month of June is slipping away. We are supposed to be in the Rio by July 1st. Falling behind schedule, we continued on this morning to Xcalak (pronounced Ish-ca-lak) to check out of Mexico. We pulled up to the dock in the middle of a torrential downpour, and I decided not to take my camera to shore.

"You'll be sorry," said John. "Whenever you don't take your camera, you regret it."

Xcalak is certainly one of the shabbiest little towns we have seen yet. It had a deserted feel, with only a few

run-down buildings. The weather may have had
something to do with it. The police station was an old
building, distinctive with the light from a police car on
the roof.

We were directed to the *Capitania de Puerto*, or Harbor
Master's office. Jorge Ivan Avila Morales, believe it or
not, is the same guy who held the job 10 years ago when
our cruising guide was written.

I felt like we were on a set from the Andy Griffith show.
Senor Jorge pulled a squeaky old chair up to a bare,
metal desk. He inserted the form into an old fashioned
typewriter and pecked away at the keys, reminding me
of Barney Fife.

It was a breeze, compared to what we went through
when we arrived in Mexico. Nobody thumbed through
our frozen vegetables or studied the packaging on our
frozen meat.

It was certainly a far sight quicker and easier than
checking out of Cuba. Nobody gave a damn if some
Mexican wanted to hide in our boat and get away to
Belize.

So, as quietly as we came into Xcalek, we left her. It
must have been our quickest landfall yet. We didn't
shop. We didn't eat. It was the first place that I didn't
take a single photograph. And John was right. When I
saw the police station with the old light from a police
car on the roof, I did regret not bringing my camera to
shore.

The marina we stayed at in Isla Mujeres

A Mexican official at Isla Mujeres

Diamond Lil, in her slip at Isla Mujeres

John, on the *Malecon* in Isla Mujeres

Isla Mujeres street

Seaside dining in Isla Mujeres

John, relaxing in Isla Mujeres

Diamond Lil, at our Marina in Isla Mujeres

John, looking dashing in his new hat

The tuna that John caught on the way to Cozumel

John,driving the dinghy in Cozumel.

Diamond Lil, anchored in front of Cozumel, Mexico

A fleet of colorful water taxis in Cozumel

Dressed for the sun in Cozumel

Diamond Lil, tied up at the fuel dock at Puerto Aventuras Marina

Looking out at the cut from the sea to Puerto Aventuras

Our slip at Puerto Aventura Marina

Watching the Swim with the Dolphins show at Puerto Aventuaras

A close up shot of the dolphins at Puerto Aventuras

Condominiums behind the marina

Heading towards Punta Allen, Mexico

John, re-attaching the anchor after it came lose in rough seas

A visit from the Mexican Navy, way out on the Chinchorro Banks

And there they go...............

Chapter 4

Belize

June 29, 2007

Exotic is the word that first comes to mind when I attempt to describe San Pedro, on Ambergris Caye, Belize. It was our first stop in Belize and our check-in point. By the time we got the dinghy to shore it was almost 5:00 pm. The immigration officer gave us forms to fill out and told us to come back in the morning.

We arrived bright and early but found that the officer had gone to the airport to process several officials arriving for a meeting of the leaders of several Central American countries, including the President of Mexico. We received another handful of forms from the customs officer and filled them out while we waited for him to return. We waited and waited, along with many others and the captain was getting a little agitated and irritated after a while. Finally the ordeal was over and we were legal. Unlike Cuba and Mexico, there were no check-in charges; although apparently there is a small exit charge. We explored the streets of this fascinating little town. San Pedro is the main tourist center in Belize and there was plenty of activity, as people buzzed along the narrow streets in their golf carts.

English is the official language of Belize although we hear about 50/50 English and Spanish in the streets. We were very lucky to arrive on *Dia de San Pedro*, a tribute to their Patron Saint Peter, which is celebrated with a four-day long bash. There was a little fair, lots of entertainment, fireworks etc. We are exhausted from our last few days of traveling. We enjoyed the sights by day and were quite content to listen to the sounds of the vibrant nightlife through our open hatch.

The anchorage is protected by a reef which stops the waves but not the wind. The holding is great and our anchor is buried deep, thankfully, because the wind has howled since we arrived. Boats, including fast ferries whiz by constantly, which makes for a very choppy anchorage. We love the town but not the anchorage and after two nights are happy to be on our way. We are a little behind schedule but we're getting close.

June 30

Cruising in Belize reminds us of the Abacos in the Bahamas. Between the mainland to the west and a long series of cays to the east is a huge, protected body of water, called the Main or Inner Channel. It is along this channel that we will cruise our way south to Guatemala.

The open ocean passages are past us and we are both relieved to be in calm waters again. The channel is only about nine feet deep. Compared to over a thousand feet of the ocean we have left behind, this feels great!

There are countless cays to explore but we will only see a few as we head south. Hopefully on the return trip we will explore much more of this gorgeous cruising ground in Belize.

We passed Belize City, having heard that it is dirty and dangerous and continued five miles southwest of the big city to Cucumber Marina. The marina is named after a Florida resident who set up here in the 1950's, growing vegetables, including cucumbers and exporting them from this port.

It is a charming marina with tight security. We have seen several guards armed with rifles walking around. We are one of three Canadian boats in a row on the dock here. I did the laundry while John washed the salt off the boat and I set to work catching up on our latest adventures. Tomorrow we will continue south and in just two to three days we hope to be in Guatemala.

July 1

Planning to stop for one last night in Belize, we dropped anchor by the charming seaside village of Placencia. It was the most comfortable anchorage we have found so far on this trip and we agreed almost immediately that although we were a mere 51 nautical miles from Guatemala, we would stay here and rest for a couple of days.

Paradise was the word that came to mind when we stepped ashore, confirming our decision to spend a couple of days here. Off in the distance we can just make out the peaks of the Cockscombe range of the Maya Mountains reaching up into the clouds. Placencia is on the southern tip of an elongated peninsula with a long, crescent shaped beach on the ocean side.

Colorful homes and guest cottages are built up on stilts to catch the cool Caribbean trade winds. The main thoroughfare through town is a narrow, mile-long sidewalk that took nearly 30 years to complete. We walked till we dropped, enjoying the brilliant tropical flowers and trees in full bloom, some of which we have never seen before.

On the other side of the peninsula is the entrance to the Placencia Lagoon, which provides protection in stormy weather. We discovered that we could check out of Belize in the little town of Mango Creek, just across the lagoon and up the Mango River, a short twenty-minute dinghy ride.

On our second day we set off with a full tank of gas and all our paperwork to find the immigration office. Somewhere along the way we made a wrong turn and drove for many miles through mangrove lined waterways that snaked like a maze towards the mountains.

Our twenty-minute ride took a couple of hours. Luckily, we came across a father and his two sons cutting some poles out of the thick undergrowth, and asked for directions. The looks on their faces told us we had gone way past our cut-off, so we retraced our path and eventually discovered where we had gone wrong.

Arriving in the little Creole community of Independence/Mango Creek, we tied up beside a fishing boat and asked the first person we saw for directions to the immigration office. He walked over to his pickup truck and gestured for us to get in. He drove us to the office, which was 2 ½ miles away. We were thankful for the ride because we were already sunburned and hot from our long dinghy ride. It is always interesting to travel further inland than our feet will take us and to see a town that is not geared towards tourists.

The clearing out process only took about five minutes, cost $15.00 Belize ($7.50 U.S.) and best of all involved NO new paperwork. We asked how long we could stay once we were cleared out and received a very vague "no problem" as an answer. It was a breeze. We were returned to our dinghy and as we passed the fishing boat we noticed a nice pile of lobster tails on ice. We bought 1 lb. for $25.00 Belize (12.50 U.S,) and for that we received three medium-sized and one large tail, enough for a feast.

Placencia is the Belizean base for the Moorings Charter Company. There are currently 17 of their boats anchored here along with few private boats and *Diamond Lil*. We are the token Canadians.

Sailors fly in from all over the world to cruise the beautiful waters of Belize, with its hundreds of cays and interesting mainland destinations to explore, everything from Mayan ruins to jungle trips.

We picked up a fresh pineapple from a little stand on the side of the road in town, after smelling the sweet aroma from about 20 feet away. We enjoyed seared jerk tuna (from our catch back near Cozumel) and added the fresh pineapple at the last minute. It was the most delicious pineapple we have ever tasted. I have already planned a return trip to the same stand for a few veggies, some oranges and a mango.

I enjoyed a little fishing from the swim platform yesterday and landed a little squirrel fish. Something big chased him up though so I think I'll try again later. A couple on a sailboat named *Barnacle* just up-anchored from beside us in the anchorage and pulled away.

 I wonder if they too, are headed for the Rio Dulce. The captain has gone to shore for some ice and we promise ourselves that we will definitely leave tomorrow. *Manana*.

San Pedro, on Ambergris Caye, Belize

San Pedro beachside bar

The beautiful, white sand beach of San Pedro

The Belize Coast Guard was in full force

Security was high due to a meeting of Central American leaders

San Pedro street

Diamond Lil, in our slip at Cucumber Beach Marina, Belize

The Cucumber Beach Restaurant and Bar

Out on the sea – heading from Cucumber Beach to Placencia, Belize

Heading into Placencia in the dinghy from our anchorage

The charming walkway through Placencia

Placencia

Colorful Placencia home

Catching catfish in Placencia

Chapter 5

Rio Dulce, Guatemala,

July 5, 2007

There were times when it seemed like we would never get here and times that I felt like turning around and heading back, but I'm happy to say that we are finally here! It took us three weeks and two days to reach the Rio Dulce from where we set off, in Marathon. However, we stopped to enjoy many places along the way.

We experienced a lot of bumpy rides even though the weather wasn't bad. As we traveled from north to south, the prevailing winds from the east caused waves to hit us in the side pretty well the entire way from Isla Mujeres.

Out of necessity, we devised a method of power tacking, heading first into the wind and then letting it carry us from behind, rather than taking it in the side which is most uncomfortable. It adds a few extra miles to our route, but made for a much more pleasant ride.

Upon arrival in Guatemala, the instructions in our cruising guide recommended that we drop anchor in front of Livingston. However, the book also warned of poor holding, strong currents, and uncomfortable sea swells, which was an understatement.

We opted instead to tie off along the dock at *La Marina,* with hopes of finding a water taxi to take us back into town, since conditions were far too rough to launch our dinghy.

There was no response from *La Marina* to our call on
the VHF radio, nor was there any sign of the restaurant,
bar, or hot showers that the guide described. We
wandered around the deserted marina grounds, looking
for someone who could tell us whether it was all right to
leave our boat while we checked in. But there was no
sign of life. A helpful man from the property next door
offered to take us to town in his boat, a sturdy fiberglass
runabout.

In our broken Spanish, we arranged for him to pick us
back up in *dos horas* (two hours). Checking in was a
breeze in Livingston compared to Cuba, Mexico, and
Belize, probably due to the number of cruisers who come
here for hurricane season. After exploring the town, we
found our ride back to *Diamond Lil*.

When John asked the man how much we owed him for
the ride, he replied, "whatever," - the only English word
I heard him use. His response of *"bueno"* to our payment
of 50 *quetzales*, approximately $6.67 U.S., was
appreciated, since "whatever" was difficult to interpret,
being new to the country and currency and
unaccustomed to the expectations.

We felt a great sense of satisfaction as we replaced our
quarantine flag with the Guatemalan courtesy flag, and
entered the enchanting Rio Dulce. This would be the
last leg of our trip and the climax of our challenging
trip. We have asked much of our trusty little vessel over
the last several weeks, and she has not let us down.

We had read the famous quote by John Lloyd Stephens
about the trip up the Rio Dulce over and over. We first
found it in our cruising guide. My daughter, Sylvia, gave
me a book on Guatemala, and we found the same quote.
It describes the Rio better than I ever could.

"In a few moments we entered the Rio Dulce. On each side, rising perpendicularly from three to four hundred feet, was a wall of living green. Trees grew from the water's edge, with dense unbroken foliage, to the top ·not a spot of barrenness was to be seen; and on both sides, from the tops of the highest trees, long tendrils descended to the water, as if to drink and carry life to the trunks that bore them. It was, as its name imports, a Rio Dulce, a fairy scene of Titan land, combining exquisite beauty with colossal grandeur.

As we advanced the passage turned, and in a few moments we lost sight of the sea, and were enclosed on all sides by a forest wall; but the river, although showing us no passage, still invited us onward."

John Lloyd Stephens (1841)

Many years have passed since that was written about the Rio Dulce, but not much has changed. We read this passage many times on our way here, imagining what it would look like and we were not disappointed.

There are still little dugout *cayacos* on the river, many with just children in them, fishing with nets or marking traps with plastic pop bottles. There are also plenty of small boats with outboards like the one we rode to Livingston in. Beautiful properties with expensive yachts in covered boat slips, owned by wealthy Guatemalans, line the shore.

The river entered a small lake called El Golfete and it was here that we found a quiet little anchorage with two sailboats already settled in; safety in numbers as we had read in our cruising guide. Relieved to finally be here, we enjoyed an enchanting evening surrounded by jungle, complete with the calls of howler monkeys and the sounds of hidden night creatures.

From high in the mountains above, we could hear the sounds of people calling to each other from long distances. There are no roads here, no telephones, and no internet - just human voices, carried through the jungle. There were no lights as far as the eye could see, only a fire that a family was sitting around on shore and then the light of a lantern as they climbed up the slope to their home.

"The boat is covered in salt," I said to John. "I hope it rains hard enough to clean it off."

As my mother used to say, "Be careful what you wish for."

Never, in my life, have I ever experienced such rain. When I woke up, I snapped a picture of our dinghy, full to the brim, which shows just how much rain fell overnight.

July 6

It was no easy task to weigh anchor and leave our idyllic anchorage on the Rio Dulce. I am tired of traveling and would be content to stay here for a while but we are homeless in this strange land. Reluctantly, I agreed to continue on a little farther up the river, to look for a place to spend the next five months. We have arrived late in the season and having made no reservations, we are a little anxious to see what is available in the way of marina slips.

The skies were cloudy and it wasn't a picturesque trip. We entered what is known as the marina district of the Rio Dulce, where both sides of the river are dotted with small marinas, offering a variety of services.

We pulled into the sleepy Laguna Marina, just off the river in a peaceful lagoon. The owner was enjoying his daily siesta but another boater gave us the scoop and showed us around. At first glance it was appealing, with nice side tie versus my dreaded med-style slips, and a friendly atmosphere. However, there was no internet availability, so we cast off and resumed our search.

From the water none of the marinas looked appealing; with boats crammed in like sardines, and mostly med-style mooring which is basically an anchor out front and no dock beside the boat, just back access from the boat to the dock. That was bad enough, but the boats are crammed in so tight it looks like you could reach out and scratch your neighbor's back.

We decided to anchor in front of the town of Fronteras, also known as Rio Dulce Town, for the night in order to tune in to the morning cruiser's net to see if there were any open slips with internet access.

The anchorage is convenient to town and we took the dinghy in and tied up at Bruno's Marina, which provides a dinghy dock for all the boaters. We enjoyed a *limonada con agua,* a delicious, refreshing drink that we have discovered and ordered some lunch.

Unfortunately the Chicken Alfredo was as cold as the *limonada* and I couldn't choke mine down. I long for the delicious food we enjoyed back in Mexico and start to envision myself losing weight. There is a silver lining in every cloud, I suppose.

Our cruising guide warns of stimulation overload when stepping ashore in Fronteras and suggests visiting early in the day before the heat and odors become overwhelming. This is no exaggeration. On the west bank of the Rio, at the foot of the bridge, is the town of Fronteras. On the east bank, at the other end of the bridge, is the little town of El Relleno. Although they are sometimes referred to separately, the two towns together form what is known as Rio Dulce Town.

I was overwhelmed by the sounds of diesel air brakes from the large trucks descending the steep bridge into town. Then there was the constant honking of horns to warn pedestrians, filing along a narrow passageway between the busy roadside vendors and the traffic. The air was thick with the smells - of truckloads full of pigs and cattle passing by, of fish laid out to dry, of raw meat being sold in the shops, and of exhaust wafting up in the humid air from a steady stream of buses, trucks, cars, and motorcycles.

There is much to see and just about everything one could imagine for sale on the street, including caskets on display.

"Hey, look. Why don't you lie down in one and try it on for size?" teased John.

Armed guards stand vigil in front of banks and government buildings. Armed guards clutch on to the sides of delivery trucks, as drivers pile cases of soft drinks onto make-shift dollies. I shake my head at the need for an armed guard on a Coca-Cola truck. What kind of strange place have we landed in?

We managed to buy a Guatemalan cell phone, thanks to a helpful English speaking man standing on the street in front of his shop.

We looked at the slips at Bruno's Marina, the only marina right downtown. There is internet and a pool but the location right downtown is undesirable to us. The noise from the traffic on the bridge is constant and the proximity to town makes me nervous.

This evening, we dodged the potholes along the road, with our umbrellas clutched in our hands and returned to town, to try another meal. The rain increased in intensity as we waited for our dinner.

A waitress pointed to the ceiling above our table and then pointed to another table. I interpreted her actions as a warning that the roof above us leaked in the heavy rain. We heeded her gestured advice, and moved to the other table, which seemed to please her, and continued to wait. And wait!

Lightening lit up the anchorage in front of us and thunder shook the rickety building, as we waited for what seemed like forever. How long could it take for them to cook pizza, we wondered.

We were not encouraged about the arrival of our meal when suddenly the power went out. The entire town was in darkness. We sat for a minute, not sure what to do.

The walk to the restaurant had been challenging enough in the light of day. Even then, the water had run over the top of our feet at times. The footing was treacherous, with uneven curbs, huge pot-holes, and numerous dangers lurking along the way.

I didn't relish the walk back in even heavier rain and pitch blackness. The waitress promised, I think, that the power would be back on in *un momento*.

And it was. Our pizza finally came. Mine came about ten minutes before John's, but finally we were both fed and made it safely back to the boat. Another night of torrential rain meant sleeping with the boat closed up tight. Two fans, plugged into an extension cord and powered by our inverter brought relief from the oppressive heat.

Our quarantine flag is flying as we near Livingston, Guatemala

Diamond Lil, docked at La Marina, in Livingston, Guatemala

94

The immigration office in Livingston

Livingston, Guatemala

Heading back to *Diamond Lil* after checking in – John is all smiles

The stunning scenery as we headed up the Rio Dulce

The legendary Rio Dulce

This shows how much rain fell on our first night in the Rio

Around every bend, more beauty!

The calm bay where we anchored on our first night in Guatemala

Diamond Lil, at the dock at Laguna Marina

El Castillo de San Felipe – at the entrance to Lago Izabal

Bruno's dinghy dock

John, enjoying a cold *limonada* at Bruno's Restaurant

Chapter 6

Mario's Marina

July 7, 2007

We announced our arrival on the morning cruisers' net and were welcomed to the Rio Dulce by the host of the radio show. We mentioned that we were looking for a slip, preferably side-tie, with internet access. Two people replied that their marina had a slip available. One was Bruno's, but we agreed last night that we didn't want to be right downtown.

The other marina was Mario's. We hopped in the dinghy and were there in no time. It was 9:00 am on a Saturday morning. The weekly "swap meet" was well underway. The Cayuco Club was buzzing with activity.

We pushed our way through the crowds of boaters congregated at the bar. The pizza and Bloody Marys served on Saturday morning are a big hit.

Throughout the restaurant, tables are heaped with treasures from the bilge. Boaters bring items they want to sell or trade and prospective buyers come to browse. Local vendors set up displays of beautiful hand woven fabrics, jewelry, and crafts for everyone to admire, and hopefully buy.

Feeling a little shy, we browsed through the heaps and piles of boat stuff that we have no room for. In fact, I could picture a table heaped with stuff I'd like to get OFF our boat. We mingled with the crowd and ordered a frosty *limonada* before asking about the slip.

"Oh, you must be the couple we heard on the radio this morning," a tall woman replied.

"Hi, I'm Trish, and this is my husband, Bob," the woman said, gesturing towards the fellow sitting on the bar stool beside her. She was thin as well as tall, with close-cut reddish- blonde hair and oval shaped wire-rimmed glasses. Bob looked a little shorter, although it was hard to tell for sure since he was sitting down. He also wore wire-rimmed glasses and seemed a bit shy. We introduced ourselves, feeling a little shy, too.

"That is our boat, *Barnacle*," said Trish, as she pointed to a large sailboat, docked right in front of the Cayuco Club.

"We saw your boat a couple of days ago, in Placencia," I replied. I was right when I guessed that the couple on *Barnacle* was headed for the Rio.

"Come, I'll introduce you to Mister Jim," said Trish, leading us through the crowd, to where a group of people stood talking.

As we reached the group, a tall, good-looking man of middle age, smiled our way. He wore his medium brown hair fairly short and had strong, angular features.

"Jim, this is John and Melanie. They're the people who were asking about a slip on the radio this morning," said Trish.

The crowd seemed to quiet just a little as people turned to inspect the newcomers in their midst. A hush went through the group, but then the chatter resumed. Before

long we were introduced to many of the people in the
crowd - too many to remember names, but the gesture
was warm and sincere.

Mister Jim gave us a tour of the marina and showed us
the slip - his last available one, he claimed.

We liked the place immediately and said we would be
back with *Diamond Lil* shortly. We raced back to the
anchorage in front of Bruno's, up-anchored and returned
quickly, for fear of losing the last available slip.

As we neared the marina, we agreed that the location
was perfect – close to town, and yet not too close.
Situated on a protected little bay, it would only take us
about 10-15 minutes to drive into town in the dinghy.
And yet, the sounds of the noisy bridge traffic were too
far away to hear. Our slip is a side-tie, which makes me
very happy.

Mario's Marina offers a small but attractive pool, a
great restaurant and bar with a daily happy hour, and
reasonable meal specials. A wide variety of social
activities are held here. They tell me it's the social
center of the Rio.

There is a clean laundry room and a small convenience
store on site. An armed guard patrols the marina from
dusk till dawn, shining his flashlight on all the boats,
dinghies, and motors each time he passes by.

Dockhands buzzed out to meet us, relieving us of our
dinghy to make it easier to back into the slip. They've
done this many times, I realized, as they pushed and

pulled with their little rubber boats. Most of the vessels here are sailboats and don't maneuver as easily as *Diamond Lil*, with her twin engines.

We signed a contract for one month and received our internet username and password. We faxed our signed lease to our insurance company, back in Canada, as agreed.

Laundry was first on my list of chores. When our wash-down pump hose had come unattached on our way to the Rio, a stream of water poured through our bedroom wall and all over John's hats, clothes, and books.

The carpet was soaked for days and every towel we owned was wet and stinky from soaking up the water. Since plugging in the boat, we have been running the air conditioner in our cabin as well as two fans, blasting air on the wet floor to try to dry it out.

Wet clothes, wet hats, and wet books are spread out over every possible surface to dry out. What a mess!

July 14

It's hard to believe that we arrived at Mario's Marina a week ago today. The internet here is free and works pretty well, except for when it rains or after it rains. Of course, it has rained every night since we arrived. And it has rained during many of the days also.

I am perched on my little bar stool, in front of my laptop, attempting to get online. I have a view of the empty slip beside us and beyond that, the jungle.

Each time I log onto our Bayliner Owners Club these days, we have messages from fellow Bayliner owners. Most of them are in the U.S. or Canada. Most of them never leave their marina. A few venture out for short trips around their local waterways. So, we are a great source of inspiration to our online friends.

"You people are crazy," wrote one guy on the forum.

"Don't you people ever work?" wrote another.

Our 38-foot Bayliner stands out among the row of sailboats here at Mario's Marina. The only other power boat in this 50-slip marina is a 50-foot Nordhavn from San Francisco called *La Vagabonda*.

"Most people come to the Rio Dulce on sailboats," Raul Valize had said to us, as he processed our clearance into Guatemala a couple of days ago.

"Why do they advertise that they have internet here, if it never works?" I moaned, as I tried again to connect.

Outside the boat, a friendly dockhand is making his morning rounds, bailing out all the dinghies in the marina.

He grins when he gets to our boat and puts down his bailer. Ours he empties with our handy little pump, looking as if the change from bailing is welcome. It's a great service for guests who leave their boats behind, to travel inland, because one night's rain can fill and sink a dinghy.

The assistant manager and dock master at Mario's is Marco Antonio Linares, but we just call him Marco. He is a short, friendly Guatemalan fellow who always has a big smile on his face. He speaks some English, but with a stiff accent. The way he says Meester Jeem has caught on and even the gringos use this nickname for the manager.

Meester Jeem has filed for our nine-month extension for us. Our original clearance fees of about $100.00 U.S. only allowed us to stay for three months. Since we plan to be here for a total of five months, we need the extension. We don't need nine months' extension, but that's all that is available, at an additional cost of $150.00 U.S.

We're settling in nicely here at Mario's Marina. There are usually a few boaters hanging out down at the Cayuco Club Restaurant and Bar, especially at happy hour, held each afternoon from 4:00 to 6:00 pm. The food is great, with reasonably priced daily specials.

Monday is pot-luck night. Boaters bring their own meat, which the kitchen staff grills for them. In addition, each couple brings a side dish to share, adding it to the array of delicacies spread out on a long table. We love Monday nights!

There is a movie night, a Sunday afternoon poker game, and the usual book exchange. If you follow the shady path from the Cayuco Club, you will find a common area, built in the shade of a large *palapa*. Here, people can escape the confines of their boats and watch television, read, or mingle.

There is no cable service to the slips. If we want to watch television, we can do so in the Cayuco club or here, in this breezy spot. I don't miss it at all and even John, who would normally complain, couldn't care less. I am amazed how happy my Leo the Lion is, here in the jungle!

A little further along the same shady path is our pool. Most days, after lunch, I wander down to the pool and join a group of women as they swim and chat. Our pool is not large - but the water is very, very cool – too cool for some of the girls, who squeal as they slowly ease themselves into the water. The pool is shaded by branches from enormous trees and I love to float on my back and gaze up at them. Orchids and air plants of countless varieties flourish in my little garden in the sky.

"It's Canadian water," I say to Wendy, who is also from Canada.

"It's important to stay in at least 20 minutes," Wendy instructs me. "That's how long it takes to cool down your core."

John isn't really a pool kind of guy. While I float on my back, cooling my core, he stays back at the boat, reading in peaceful, air-conditioned comfort. Sometimes, if I'm looking in the right direction, I'll see him pass by the pool area, heading back to the boat from the restaurant. They serve some decadent desserts there. His favorite is the hot fudge brownie with vanilla ice cream.

"*Como dice* brownie?" I asked the cute girl behind the counter one day.

"*Brownie*," she answered me, laughing.

"*Oh. Ok, uno brownie con heilada, por favor. Para mi esposo.*"

John runs into town in the dinghy several times a week. Once in a while I go too, but usually he goes on his own. He heads out early, when the river is calm. In the afternoon, the wind picks up and it gets choppy out there. There are water taxis available to ferry people to town and back if the weather is bad and the water is too rough.

Each Tuesday and Thursday, from 10:30 to 11:00 am, there are free Spanish lessons provided here at the Cayuco Club. These are not just free for Mario's guests, but for anyone who cares to join. We attended Professora Linda's first class this past Tuesday, along with about 28 other boaters. Our textbooks are due to be delivered to the *tienda* soon, and I can't wait.

When we first came to Mario's, I asked Meester Jeem whether there was anywhere to take a walk. Being on a peninsula, I wasn't too hopeful.

He directed me to the back of the marina property. There, hidden from sight by the dense underbrush, is a little path through the jungle. The pathway leads to a quiet little road cut into the red earth.

If you turn right when you get to the little red road, you come to the end of it before long. Another little path leads through the jungle to the small Mango Marina.

If you turn left, the rough little road leads to the small town of Esmerelda, surrounded by jungle. It is quite bizarre. It seems like a road to nowhere, but I have been told that if you follow it for a very long time, you will eventually come out to the main highway, just outside of Fronteras.

There were no vehicles traveling on the little road; just people walking and plenty of chickens, turkey, ducks, and dogs.

"Carry a big stick if you go walking," said Meester Jeem. "There are poisonous snakes and dogs and wild animals with names that I can't even pronounce".

We carried our sticks, ready to fend off the menacing gander that screeched and spat at us and a few of the less than friendly dogs. Other than that we saw nothing too frightening. I was almost a disappointed not to see a creature with a name we couldn't pronounce.

The road was flat at first, with endless stands of *sapodilla* trees stretching out on each side. The trees were being tapped during this, the rainy season, to get *chicle,* used to make chewing gum.

A pipeline snaked along one side of the road. After a few miles the hills became very steep. Surely, we kept thinking, at the top of this next hill, we'll find something. But each crest revealed yet another hill.

Finally, we turned around and headed to the boat. The heat had sapped our energy and dulled our appetite for lunch. We showered and dropped into our cool little cocoon for a very long siesta.

July 12

"This sounds like fun," I told John, as I scanned the brochure for a tourist excursion to Livingston.

"Why do you want to go there? Why take a water taxi when we have our own dinghy?" he asked, in his logical way.

"It will be fun. Look. The *panga* is full of people. First they stop at the hot springs, and then take us to Livingston. You can just relax and not worry about driving."

I loved the coastal, Garifuna community of Livingston, where we checked into Guatemala a couple of weeks ago. However, our schedule did not permit much sightseeing or shopping in the touristy little town the day we cleared through customs and immigration.

After pleading my case, we found ourselves back at the water-taxi terminal in Fronteras the next morning, along with a boatload of tourists, mostly young back-packers.

The captain rolled his eyes as we were loaded into the crowded boat, but once we were out on the river, he lost some of his crustiness and enjoyed the trip.

It was a different perspective from water level than the

one we had seen from our fly bridge the day we arrived in the Rio. The tour included several points of interest along the Rio and a stop for a dip in the hot springs along the way.

July 18

Each Wednesday, Marco drives the marina van to the nearby towns of Puerto Barrios and Morales. He picks up the mail, does the banking and shopping, and stops for lunch. There is a sign-up sheet down in the *tienda*, where anyone who wishes to accompany Marco can add their name.

It was an early start. We met at the Cayuco Club at 7:00 am and were in the *launcha* by 7:30, heading for El Relleno, the part of the town on the east side of the bridge, where the van was parked.

We drove through the lush, green Motague valley, enjoying the view of the Montanas del Mico. These are the peaks, across the Rio from the marina, that we have been gazing at since we arrived. They are small compared to some of the mountains in other parts of the country, but still very scenic.

We had breakfast in Puerto Barrios, at a very modern, clean, American-style chain restaurant. It was quite different than anything we had seen. I was surprised when we passed a McDonald's restaurant.

Our neighbor Jim, from *Oasis 1*, the boat in the slip beside us at Mario's, has come along also. We stopped

where Marco needed to. We stopped wherever Jim
needed to.

Marco led us to a store that sold toasters. John has been
looking for one in Fronteras. One day he found an
empty toaster box in a store there. The storekeeper
gestured at the empty box and told John, "*dos dias.*"

After two days John returned to the store. The
storekeeper said "*a las una.*"

So, he went back at 1:00 pm. At 1:00 pm. he told John to
come back after 2:00. John actually did go back at 2:00
and the shopkeeper said to come back at 3:00.

To this John replied, "*Manana*".

Two days later we returned and he told us *"dos dias,"* so
when we saw the toaster in Puerto Barrios, we grabbed
it. People don't eat much toast in Guatemala, according
to Marco. They are more likely to scoop their eggs up
with a tortilla, along with salsa and beans.

Puerto Barrios is described in our Guatemala guide
book as a town people don't normally visit unless they
are traveling through on their way somewhere else and
refers to it as a forlorn place. Forlorn describes it well,
but it is the closest place to buy many of the things that
the marina needs to operate.

When we left Puerto Barrios, we retraced our route and
stopped along the way in the little town of Morales,
another pretty forlorn place. Our guide book calls this
town "a ramshackle collection of wooden huts and

railway tracks that was the headquarters of the United Fruit Company" and refers to it as a squalid town. Again, only a place you pass through. Unfortunately, a blight wiped out the entire fruit crop in the area, leaving the town with virtually no economic base.

It is, however, where the marina mail is delivered and where all mail goes out. I wanted to mail a few postcards and buy some stamps and to do this we took an all-day trip. It was interesting, but I made sure that I loaded up with stamps and plan to ask Marco to drop off my postcards for me from now on.

July 24

The captain and I are getting into a groove here in Rio Dulce. The weather has improved and we have had less rain and more sunny days. I just walked up to the Cayuco Club to buy the captain a huge, decadent piece of Key lime pie for 23 *quetzals* (about $3.00).

I killed a nasty looking spider on the back deck one day. I looked it up on a website and he is a nasty bug, indeed. Its bite, although not deadly can result in a gruesome-looking open wound. We are keeping our shoes on, eyes open, and spraying often!

There is so much see here on the Rio. We have just barely scratched the surface. The Rio offers marinas of every size and shape and it is taking us quite a while to explore them all.

Directly to our east is Mango Marina. It is the only one within walking distance and doesn't offer much in the way of services. My friend Sara keeps her boat there, and I've walked over with her a few times. There is an old, once-used pool, but it stands empty and sad-looking now.

Across the *Golfete* from us, on the southern shore, is Monkey Bay Marina, which specializes in long-term storage. It has water access only, is surrounded by jungle and hasn't much in the way of facilities.

To our west, between Mario's and the town of Fronteras, is the Catamaran Island Hotel. It was the first marina to open on the river. They have a beautiful pool with a swim-up bar and a nice restaurant.

A little further to the west, just off-shore from Fronteras, is the Hacienda Tijax. It is a jungle lodge as well as a marina, located on the tip of a 50-acre rubber and teak plantation. It is an enchanting spot, and their canopy tours have been highly recommended by several of our new friends.

Of course, right in town, on the north side of the bridge, is Bruno's Marina. We spent our first night in the Rio anchored in front of Bruno's. Most everyone parks their dinghy at Bruno's dinghy dock when they go to town. We often stop at the little bar/restaurant for a drink with friends or a bite to eat. Bruno's also has a pool and a very good *tienda* on site.

Across the bridge, on the southern shore, is Mar Marine. They offer a good size restaurant/bar and have a nautical supply store on site, which we have visited several times already.

Not far from Mar Marine, in the south eastern corner of the *Golfete*, is Ram Marine. It is the newest marina on the Rio and is still under construction. It has a large, modern fuel dock and a decent store. It will be offering many services such as haul-outs and boat repairs.

Half a mile further west, upriver from the bridge, is El Tortugal Marina. This marina also has a restaurant and a good-sized library.

On the other side of the Rio, also west of the bridge, tucked away up a secluded little river, is Laguna Marina, also known as Susannah's. There is a restaurant on site, but we weren't impressed with the one meal we had there.

There is another small, new marina near Fort San Felipe called Nutria Marina.

We have been busy making the rounds, visiting each of the marinas to check out their slips and attractions. We have tried all of the restaurants. We have not found a marina where we would rather be than right here at Mario's.

Zipping across the *Golfete* in our rubber dinghy earlier today, we explored a scenic little river that runs into Monkey Bay.

Monkey Bay was named after two troops of free-ranging black howler monkeys, who can be heard from miles away. We have heard their eerie call from our boat several times, and are on a mission to find them.

The howler monkey is the loudest animal in the world, with its roar being heard over a mile away. The largest monkey found in the Americas, they have become threatened due to destruction of their rainforest habitat. The best time to hear the monkeys is at dawn but we wanted to find the spot in the daylight first. We turned the motor off and drifted. Within seconds, the jungle came alive with the buzzing and chirping of unseen creatures.

Sun dappled the lush canopy above us, as we drifted silently past the wide-reaching roots of a Ceiba tree, under broad branches bearing all sort of odd-shaped fruits and massive bromeliads. I focused on a vivid patch of purple flowering sea hyacinths, lining the shore. On and on we floated through the magical wonderland.

To my right, a virtual lawn of water plants stretched across a motionless creek leading off the Monkey River. Crisp, brown leaves lay scattered across the top of the algae-covered water. Twigs and branches poked up through the solid mass. Small patches of sun snaked their way through the dense jungle above us, casting a lacy pattern of light all around.

July 26

Two days ago, we were floating silently through an isolated jungle river. Today we saw the jungle from another angle - from a walkway suspended 60 feet above the jungle floor.

We parked our dinghy at Hacienda Tijax early this
morning and wandered up to the lobby to sign up for the
2 ½-hour hike and canopy tour. I stole a clip of John,
walking along the trail with his walking stick. On his
head is his beige Tilly hat and he wears beige shorts
with an old, faded white t-shirt.

On the front of his shirt it says - TGIF – Thank God it
Floats. He found the old shirt in a drawer *Diamond Lil*
when we bought her. It is not like John to wear another
man's old shirt, but this one was special, and he loves it.
He rolls his eyes and gives me a dirty look, so I focus on
Lucy, our tour- guide, who is a much more cooperative
subject.

As luck would have it, John and I were the only hikers
that showed up today, so we enjoyed having Lucy as our
own personal guide. She was a small woman, not much
more than five feet tall. She wore her medium brown
hair cut short. I notice as she whisks a flying ant-type
creature onto her hand that she also wears her
fingernails short – bitten short.

Lucy has on blue jean Capri pants, red sandals, and a
navy blue t-shirt with a big, white flower on the front.
She is passionate about her work. I get the feeling that
she would be out here with the jungle creatures whether
we showed up or not. She shared vast amounts of
knowledge about the rainforest with us, including the
medicinal uses of numerous tropical trees and plants.

Lucy stopped often to pick seeds or leaves for us to
smell, - wild basil, allspice seeds and leaves, and even
some putrid rubber being tapped from a rubber tree.
She pointed out tiny birds, little lizards, and all kinds of
bugs. We saw epiphytes, bromeliads, orchids, palms,
and ferns.

She spoke with a musical voice and a delightful
Guatemalan accent. As I filmed her telling us a story of
her childhood, I became enchanted by this little Goddess
of the Jungle.

"*Papo Samyo*," she said, holding the flying ant-type
thing in her hand, as she began her tale, in broken
English.

"You know, and when I was a kid, and I was living in
Guatemala City, you know the seasons were more
marked before, yeah. And, you know, in May, it would
definitely start raining. But, because of global warming,
it doesn't happen anymore. And then, you would find in
the streets, when May was coming, it would be
thousands of them, in a long line of these. And then,
when we went to school, we took a lot of these and we
would make them fight. You know, chop their heads and
everything."

No, I didn't know, I thought to myself, as I remembered
our school yard games of skipping and hop-scotch.

We hiked all the way up to the Shaman Tower, where
we enjoyed a spectacular view of the Rio Dulce and the
jungle below.

I wondered how John would fare during the canopy walk part of the hike. Long ribbons of suspended wooden walkways snaked through the jungle, 60 feet high. Two 2x8 pieces of lumber ran down the middle of the walkway, attached to a series of 2x4 pieces of lumber. Railings, fashioned from long bamboo shafts and hung at waist height, were attached with ropes. This left much of the space open, therefore you could look down - way down, as you walked.

As I walked the catwalks, I filmed the jungle below, to my sides, and even above me. I filmed the captain looking straight ahead as he hustled from platform to platform. What a trooper he is, I thought to myself, way up here, with his fear of heights.

Hot and exhausted, we arrived back at the marina, looking forward to showers and a/c, only to find the power out - a common occurrence. We cooled the boat down quickly with the generator and then headed to the pool. It's remarkable how a power outage brings the crowds out to the Cayuco Club for a cool drink and to the pool for a refreshing dip!

Tomorrow we will catch a 3:00 pm bus in Rio Dulce Town (Fronteras), which will take us to Flores, a three hour ride. From there, we will take another bus to the little town of El Remate, where we will stay at La Casa De Don David for three nights. The best part is the price – only $44.00 U.S. per night for the room, including a/c, hot water and dinner for two!

From there we will tour Tikal, the famous, 40-acre
Mayan ruins, situated right on the edge of the jungle
reserve, where wildlife is abundant.

Admiral Mel on *Diamond Lil* in our new slip at Mario's Marina

Our slip was the second one from the far end of the marina

La tienda – the store at Mario's Marina

The Cayuco Club at Mario's Marina

A tuk-tuk on the street in Fronteras

The pool at Mario's Marina

The view from the bridge, looking towards the east

Backpackers Hotel, seen from up on the bridge

Guatemalan woman

Enjoying a cold drink in Fronteras

Spanish class with Professora Linda at Mario's Marina

The road that ran through the little town of Esmerelda

Enjoying a dip in the hot springs on our way to Livingston

Seeing the sights in Morales, Guatemala

A beautiful jungle river we explored in our dinghy

The scenery was equally spectacular above our heads

John, walking along one of many hanging walkways above the jungle

A view of the Rio from the Shaman Tower at Tija

Chapter 7

El Remate and Tikal, Guatemala

July 30, 2007

"You simply must take some of the land trips," echoed our fellow cruisers at Mario's. After several seasons on the Rio, they were anxious to share their "land trip" experiences with us and make suggestions and recommendations of destinations, lodgings, and activities. After 2 ½ years of living aboard, planning a land trip was now as exciting as planning boat trips once was.

Of all the land trips available in Guatemala, the one our friends insisted we take was the trip to the famous ruins at Tikal, the birthplace of the Mayas. There are hotels right at Tikal, but they are more expensive, we are told, and there are several other places to stay, nearby.

Some of our friends suggested we stay at Flores, a beautiful spot, but a little far from Tikal. Had we decided to stay in Flores we would have been picked up for our tour of Tikal at 4:00 am, which was a tad early for even us boaters. The objective when visiting Tikal is to arrive as early as possible in the morning, in order to beat the heat and the crowds and to enjoy the early morning sounds of the jungle.

Other friends suggested the peaceful little town of El Remate. Closer to Tikal, their tour departed at 5:30 am, a whole hour and a half later. The price of the excursion included a guided tour of Tikal, transportation to and from the park, and a boxed lunch.

Traveling 200 kilometers north by bus towards El Remate, we enjoyed a marvelous view as we relaxed in air-conditioned comfort. We rested our heads on crisp, clean seat covers as our shiny red *Linea Dorada* bus climbed up and down the steep hills, winding through the mountainous countryside. Miles of pastureland whizzed by, with stretches of jungle in between. Mile after mile of living fences zipped past. Instead of plain posts like we use back in Canada, fence wire here is strung along living, red-barked trees, which grow over the years, providing a scenic background.

Now and then we passed through small towns. Flat-roofed, one-story buildings line the road on both sides. Most of them are made from cement and are painted bright colors. The nicer homes have cement walls around their yards, with the color of the wall matching that of the home. The not-so-nice ones have rusty sheet metal roofs. Most have broad overhangs, for shade from the blistering sun.

At the town of St. Helena, the buildings are similar, but there are more of them and they're further back from the road, with parking lots; most of them dirt, but a few paved. Little dirt side streets run off the main road. Fruit and vegetable vendors line the road for several blocks, their crates of brightly colored produce stacked under makeshift canopies. Small, red, three-wheeled tuk-tuks share the street with bicycles, cars, trucks, and buses. In St. Helena, we transferred to a second, smaller bus, which took us into the town of Flores.

In Flores, the scenic, lake-side town we had heard so much about, we were herded with great haste into a third bus - a small van called a *tourismo*. I had no time to film the sights. Finally, after a very long day of traveling, the *tourismo* took us the last 37 kilometers to El Remate.

El Remate, situated on the eastern shore of Lago Petén Itza, in the state of Petén, was barely on the map until 1951, when the Guatemalan government built an airstrip there. This allowed archeologists, as well as tourists, accessibility to Tikal for the first time. The boost to tourism in the area has resulted in a paved road and the most modern electrical wiring that we have seen since we left the U.S.

Petén is the second largest state in the country and is believed to be both the birthplace and the heartland of the Mayan civilization. It covers approximately one third of Guatemala and yet contains just over three percent of the population. Unlike other parts of the country, there are still vast areas of land totally untouched by man in Petén.

Our *tourismo* came to a stop in front of La Casa de Don David. The charming resort had been recommended by several of our fellow cruisers. We were checked in and briefed on the tour the next morning. Then we were led down a set of steps to room #9.

"They can't be serious," I grumbled to the captain as I unpacked. It sounded like they were operating a daycare center above us. The sound of little feet running back and forth echoed through the room.

"I was hoping for a little peace and quiet. This isn't what we escaped the steamy Rio for," I complained.

"We are right below the restaurant and it doesn't stay open late. Don't worry – they will all go home before we go to bed," said John, trying to cheer me up.

"Let's hope so. But maybe they won't. Maybe they'll be there at 6:00 am for breakfast. Why don't I see if we can change rooms before we get unpacked?" I suggested.

Climbing up the steps to the office, I explained, as best I could, in Spanish, that we would like a quieter room. John was waiting when I returned, shaking his head, but once we were led to room #2, he agreed. It was much more private and much quieter. I twirled around the room, with my arms stretched out at my sides.

"We have so much space," I said. "We even have our own little porch, with a table, chairs, and hammock. I love it here!"

"You love it everywhere," laughed John.

"Yes. But isn't it nice, to get away like this; to travel somewhere new?" I asked him.

I really felt like I was on a holiday as we wandered along the roadway through town and then along the lakefront. The water near the shore was shallow and dotted with hundreds of white rocks. Horses, pigs and goats graze freely everywhere - along the roadsides, on front lawns, in soccer fields and basketball courts. A few horses were tethered but most wandered freely and traffic simply went around them if the animals were on the road.

People and livestock share the lake as well. We watched women wade in to wash their laundry alongside horses drinking the fresh water. A foal ran along behind his mother, as she was led to the lake to drink. I felt for the mare for she was bone thin, with jutting hip bones. Then I spied another mare, a grey one, who was so far along with foal that she was as wide as she was tall. In all my life, some of which was spent working on a broodmare farm, I have never seen such a sight.

"Surely she must be carrying twins," I said to John.

Following the rocky pathway from the lake to the road, we passed a woman and three small children, singing and clapping. The woman was standing in the shade under a tree, facing the children - two girls and one boy. The children sat on the ground, performing.

I could not resist filming the touching scene. At first the children shied from the camera, looking to the woman for direction. She smiled and continued singing. The children picked up the pace and performed for my camera. It is a treasured clip.

July 31

The guest house lobby was dark and deserted when we left our room and stumbled up the steps. Sitting on a table was a carton with four boxed lunches inside. It looked like we had company on our tour, as we were hustled to the van and told where to sit. By 6:00 am, we were at the park.

We searched the parking lot, and before long found our guide, Juan. He had come highly recommended, especially by the women at the marina.

"He was excellent," Wendy had chuckled, "and really cute, too."

He wore a dark bandana over his forehead. His cool, red shades were pulled up over the bandana. He sported a bright red sports jersey with white stripes on the sleeves and long, navy-blue pants, also striped with white.

Dreadlocks hung down his back almost to his waist. He wasn't a black man, though – more Hispanic in looks, I'd say. The two or three day growth of black whiskers gave him a swarthy look. When he smiled, he flashed brilliant, white teeth and his dark brown eyes sparkled. Even his accent was cute. Yes Wendy – you were right.

I had been told to start early, at all costs. But, Juan explained, we were waiting for some others to arrive. Meantime, perhaps some in the group might like something to eat.

All we wanted was to get started - early. But a few of the younger people in the group were hungry and wanted food. We wandered over to a large building and bought bottles of water, waiting patiently for the others to eat. Then they had to use the washroom.

Finally, the stragglers arrived and we were off, walking along a shady path through the jungle. The air buzzed with the chorus of jungle creatures – insects, I supposed.

Our first stop was under a huge Ceiba tree. Juan explained the significance of the tree.

"Now – ah – for those of you coming from Casa Don David – the big Gods carved at the entrance come from the single log of a Ceiba tree," he said.

"Ceibas are native to Africa so probably really ancient birds introduced them to this country in a migration a long time ago, or maybe space ships, or something like that," Juan continued, getting a few laughs from the crowd.

Towering above the rainforest, Tikal is known to be the most magnificent of all Mayan sites and is the prime attraction for tourists visiting Petén. Surrounding Tikal is the 160,000 square kilometer *Reserva de la Biosfera Maya*, the largest tropical forest reserve in Central America. The area is rich in wildlife, including over 285 species of birds, tapirs, ocelots, deer, coatis, jaguars, monkeys, crocodiles, snakes, insects, and butterflies.

The sheer size of the ruins of Tikal leaves a lasting impression. The Central area, which took us approximately five hours to explore on foot represents only about three square miles of a total 22 square mile area. Satellite imagery detects approximately 10,000 structures, with about 4,000, including temples, palaces, engraved rocks, and ball game courts found in the Central area. Half of this Central area is open to visitors.

The pyramids of Tikal are considered one of the seven wonders of the modern world and are a UNESCO World

Heritage Site. There are seven sets of twinned pyramids at the site, an archeological feature found only in the Tikal region. Civilization existed at Tikal between the years of 700 BC to 900 AD, with a population of 150,000 at the peak of its existence.

.

The climax of the tour was an up-close howler monkey sighting. Juan performed an impressive monkey call, more like a deep growl. The huge, hairy black beast in the trees above our heads growled back. At times it sounded more like a huge dog or a big tiger than a monkey. But it hung in the trees and wound its tail around limbs just like a monkey. It performed for us for 20 or 30 minutes before we continued on our tour.

We walked many, many miles and I climbed to the top of one pyramid and two temples. I counted over 100 steps on just one of my climbs. John was quite happy to remain on the ground and chat with Juan.

The temples are numbered in the order that they were discovered, not the order they were built or the order they are seen when touring the site. Fortunately, we were shaded by the jungle most of the time, making it much cooler than we had expected.

Walking through the scenic town of El Remate on Lago Peten Itza

La Casa de Don David – our hotel in El Remate

As soon as I agreed to look at one child's wares, they all swarmed me

The North Acropolis, part of the Great Plaza, built in 700 AD

Temple IV, from a distance

The view from the top of Temple IV, the highest at 236 feet

Some of the members of our group, with Juan (right)

The howler monkey we saw on our Tikal tour

Chapter 8

Guatemala City and Antigua

August 25, 2007

We're enjoying our second excursion into Guatemala's interior. The first stop on our itinerary is Guatemala City or "the city," as they say here. We plan to spend a few days here, shopping for a new laptop, before continuing to Antigua.

Marco ferried us by *launcha* over to Fronteras at 7:00 am. We bought our tickets and stood waiting for the 7:45 am bus on the noisy, dusty street with crowds of Guatemalans. I begged for the window seat, always eager to see and film new sights. The bus ride is a bargain at 50 *quetzals* each (about $7.00 U.S.).

Guatemala City is totally different than any of the places we have visited in the country. It has a population of about three million people, making it about the size of Toronto. It is made up of various zones, or *zonas*, sprawled out in all directions.

The taxi ride to the hotel cost another 50 Q, including tip. *Las Torres* Guest House in *Zona* 10 comes very highly recommended by our fellow cruisers back in the Rio. It is a lovely area with a good selection of large, modern hotels.

Las Torres is not quite as lovely, and nothing about it is modern. It's a much older building - so old that it appears that the other buildings have built up around it over the years.

We climb a few steps and pass an armed security guard, who is somewhat casual. His shirt looks like the top part of a uniform, but with it he wears blue jeans. The lobby is dark and dingy, but refreshingly cool. On one wall is a large map of the city and below it a bulletin board full of boat cards.

I film the scene, including a close-up of the bulletin board. Then I add our *Diamond Lil* boat card and film another clip, zooming in it. Now, other boaters who pass this way will see our card and know that we too, were here.

Our room at Las Torres Guest House only cost us $25.00 per night, including free internet, although we have to walk downstairs to use it. As we are led to a room, I can see why the price is so low. We pass through a strange little common area, where a coffee machine is set up, and down a narrow hallway.

The walls are cement and painted yellow. Brown parquet covers the floors. We pass the little internet station, no more than three tiny cubicles off to one side of the hallway. My reflection, filming our walk through the weird place, is caught in a large, wall-sized mirror at the end of the long hall.

We turn to the right at the mirror and follow another narrow hallway, stopping outside a strange looking room. It resembled a jail cell more than a hotel room. It had no windows and the door to the hallway was a flimsy old shower door, which didn't even lock.

I was thankful for our sessions with Professora Linda as I piped up with "*Un otro cuarto, por favor. Con una ventana* (another room please, with a window)."

It worked. The woman closed the shower door to the jail cell and led us back to the lobby. She consulted her notes and retrieved a new key from the pigeon holes built into the wall behind her.

Back we went, through the maze of hallways, and then up a long, circular cement stairway. Our footsteps echoed like we were walking through an old castle. The woman opened another door. This room was way off in a funny corner of the funny building, but it had a window and a proper door that locked.

I gave the room a quick inspection. The fridge was decent and the bathroom was clean. The shower worked. And we had a window. It was the type of window where small, horizontal glass sections open out, so you can see between them, from the right angle. Then, beyond the glass was a grid of iron bars that you had to peek through.

It was probably just as well, I thought, trying to position my video camera between the little horizontal panes of glass as well as the iron bars, to shoot some video of our view.

From the second floor, we peered down over much of the one-story building. Below us was a patchwork roof of sheet metal, in various stages of rusting. An equally mismatching grid of white plumbing pipes snaked up and down the walls and over the roof.

Third-world wiring ran down the walls in full view and lay in clusters all over the sheet metal roof. The walls surrounding the small grounds were topped with prison-style circular barbed-wire. Nice!

"We are here at the Las Torres Guest House," I narrated, as I filmed. "This is the view from our window. Not fancy but it sure sounds nice."

The trees below were alive with a symphony of raucous birdsong. It reminded of me of the sounds I heard when I passed the trees just outside Bruno's Marina in Fronteras. The trees beside the steps you walk down to get to Bruno's parking lot; the steps that always smell like piss.

As I looked beyond the barbed wire, where the tall Holiday Inn Hotel looms, I realized that I preferred our bizarre little room to one of those sterilized, high-rise suites where the windows don't even open and the sounds of life outside are drowned out by the hum of an air conditioner.

"You must eat at *Hacienda Real*," my friend Jeanie had told me. It's fabulous and just a short walk from *Los Torres*."

Of all the restaurants we have ever visited, Hacienda Real will always stand out in my mind as the most romantic. I was enveloped in the atmosphere immediately, as a handsome young host led us through the lobby and to our table.

Romantic dining areas were separated by low brick walls and giant ferns and tropical plants. A trio of musicians roamed from table to table, dressed in matching black tuxedos with black bow ties, strumming their acoustic guitars and singing sweet, Spanish love songs.

We were doted on from the moment we arrived. I couldn't count the number of handsome young servers, identically dressed in black trousers, long-sleeved white shirts and black vests, bowing and bending and catering to our every whim. Each one had tied around his waist a crisp, white, floor-length apron.

Within moments of being seated, two mugs of delicious, steaming broth were set before us. A small earthenware vessel, known as a fire pot, was positioned nearby. Inside the clay chamber a glowing bed of charcoal warmed us from the chilling mountain air.

Our friends had recommended the steak diner, and we were not disappointed as we savored the tastiest meal in recent memory.

August 26

"The city" is apparently where people from all over Central America come to shop and do business. One of the reasons we are here is to buy a new laptop. Our old one has died. We are looking for an English language model, which is apparently not easy to find in Guatemala.

The climate up in the highlands is totally different from that of the Rio Dulce. It is refreshingly cool and we have yet to see a single person on the streets wearing shorts. Most are wearing long sleeves and jackets. I can't believe that I am admitting this but it is nice to have cooler weather for a change. The humidity and heat in the Rio Dulce is constant and stifling.

After walking the streets for hours, searching through different stores, trying to communicate in Spanish, we found a new English language model laptop - and at a good price. It was quite a challenge purchasing it entirely in Spanish, but we managed.

John doesn't care for the city and is anxious to leave. So, tomorrow we are planning to head a little further west, to spend a few days in Antigua. It was the capital of Guatemala before Guatemala City. It's a much more scenic city and one of the top tourist attractions in the country.

August 27

Leaving behind the hustle and bustle of modern Guatemala City, we headed for the old colonial city of Antigua. I was under the assumption that we would be riding in one of the nicer, air-conditioned tourist buses so it came as a surprise when the taxi pulled into a station full of the brightly colored chicken buses that we had heard much about. We were quickly herded onto one, as if there was no time to lose. I felt uneasy, watching from my window as a man tossed our bags on top of the bus, well out of sight. I purposely chose the front seat, directly behind the driver, for a great view of the ride.

It seems that the objective of the chicken bus is to pack as many people as possible on to the bus in as short a time as possible and race as fast as possible along the route. These drivers are not paid by the hour and each one has a partner who stands on the bottom step leaning out the open doorway, casing the roadsides for prospective passengers.

"Antigua, Antigua, San Lucas, San Lucas, Antigua" our driver shouted along the way, attempting to lure riders. When a prospective passenger is spotted, the bus screeches to a stop, barely long enough for the poor soul to climb aboard, and then peels off again. The driver does not wait patiently for riders to take their seat or accelerate gently, like we are used to. Time is money here and these guys waste no time.

There are buses everywhere, all swerving in and around each other to gain a few seconds. Horns fill the air. Our bus had a really loud air horn that the driver leaned on frequently, blending nicely with the loud Spanish music playing on the radio.

At one point our driver stomped on the brakes, burning rubber and sending people lurching around the bus, as he stopped for a last minute passenger.

At a busy bus stop, a vendor hops on to the bus, peddling his wares to the riders - small pieces of fruit in clear plastic bags. He works his way to the back of the bus. As it slows, he hops out the back door. I look up and another vendor has hopped on. This one has candy and hats for sale. The next one has ice cream. Here you can shop and never have to leave the bus.

Our hair-raising chicken bus ride ended as we arrived at a dusty bus station in a not-so-nice part of town. Diesel fumes choked me as I was herded off. The driver was in as much of a hurry as when he herded us on. Brightly colored buses were parked everywhere. We wove our way around them, searching in every direction for some indication of which way we should go.

Our plan was to walk a short distance to the tourist office, located centrally alongside the *Parque*, which marks the center of town. There are many hotels available, in every price range, we had been told. Surely it wouldn't be that difficult to find a place to stay.

I felt like we were contestants in some kind of reality

show. We were quite a sight, pulling our bright red gringo suitcases along the cobblestone streets, hauling them up and down steep curbs and obstacles along the way.

We rolled our bags around a body sprawled out on the ground. My first thought was that he was passed out drunk, but as we practically stepped over him, I noticed that a pool of blood was forming under him.

"John. He's hurt. Maybe we should stop and help him," I said, pausing slightly, but John hurried me along.

He pointed to the security guards, standing off to one side.

"It looks like this just happened, Mel. Just keep going. You don't want to get mixed up in this. We just scream tourist, carrying two laptops, one still brand new in the box, and wheeling bright red luggage. Just keep walking."

We made our way to the tourist office. With armfuls of pamphlets, we continued on our hunt for a nice room, at a reasonable rate. It was a daunting task – weaving up and down busy cobblestone streets, laden down with luggage. At each place, I would go in and look, while John stayed with the bags, since my Spanish is a little better. When we got to Posada San Sebastian, I quickly ran out to the street and sent John up to second my vote for the room I had just fallen in love with.

August 29

Antigua became the third capital of Guatemala in 1541 and held the title until 1773, when a series of earthquakes lasting a year caused such extensive damage that the decision was made to move the capital to the site of present day Guatemala City.

Antigua was the heart of colonial power in Central America at its peak in the middle of the eighteenth century with the construction of numerous palaces, churches, monasteries, schools, and hospitals.

Today, Antigua is a cosmopolitan mix of wealthy Guatemalans who have escaped the rat race in Guatemala City to live here, those who travel the short distance to spend weekends here, tourists from all over the world, students attending the many world renowned language schools, and locals selling souvenirs.

Parque Central is the main plaza, surrounded by beautiful old buildings, lush with exotic plants and trees and complete with a risqué fountain. In the past the plaza would have been used as a market and cleared at times for bull fights, floggings, and public hangings.

There are no street signs permitted, which makes it a little difficult to find your way around. At first glance down a street there seems to be nothing but empty walls. But as you walk the street and look closer you discover large, wide-open gates and smaller doorways that lead into every kind of store, business, hotel, restaurant, and home that you could imagine.

The lack of signs on the street or store front windows results in an aesthetically pleasing look, with no commercial garishness. At night, huge heavy doors are pulled closed and locked. There seems to be a paint color code here – for the buildings wear matching shades of only a few colors; mostly earthy shades of rust, gold and brown.

Two main landmarks prevent us from getting lost. To the north is the *Cerro de la Cruz*, the Hill of the Cross and to the south the Volcano Agua. Each day at 10:00 am and 3:00 pm, the *Policia Tourisma* leads a group of tourists up the *Cerro de la Cruz* for a spectacular view of the city below. The captain chose to explore at street level, while I made the climb, always in search of great photo opportunities. I was not disappointed, as I gazed down at the city's sixteenth century Renaissance grid-pattern, far below.

August 30

The colonial town of Antigua is high on the list of the country's tourist attractions and climbing the active Pacaya Volcano was equally high on the list of what to do once we were there. Pacaya, one of Guatemala's three highly active cones, rises to a height of 2,250 meters.

Our friends, Wendy and Graham, from back at Mario's Marina, had climbed Pacaya on their visit to Antigua and encouraged us not to miss this once in a lifetime opportunity.

The weather in Guatemala is as diverse as the landscape and we had been transported from the oppressive heat, humidity, and torrential rains of the Rio in rainy season to a highland paradise much more deserving of the "land of eternal spring" title that we had heard describe Guatemala when researching the country.

We were advised to pack warm clothing for the much cooler temperatures in the highlands. I had dug out these items from the depths of our forward hatch storage. We dressed for our excursion layered in t-shirts, sweatshirts, and rain wear. We wore jeans, socks, and shoes for the first time since our last trip to Canada.

Armed with bottles of water and boxed lunches in the knapsack on my back and my trusty hands- free waist pouch where I carry my cameras, we set off from Antigua and traveled towards and along the western outskirts of the nation's capital of Guatemala City.

Our drive would take an hour and a half, each way. Our three-kilometer, guided hike would take about five hours. The climb up would take two hours. We would have about an hour to spend at the top of Pacaya. The climb down would take another two hours. For all this, the cost is a mere $7.00 U.S., each.

Once again, we snagged the front seat of the bus, with me at the window - my favorite spot for filming our adventures. Part of the excitement of any Guatemalan tour is the bus ride there and back and I love to have an up close view as the driver navigates traffic like a stock car on a race track, passing slower vehicles at every possible opportunity, uphill, downhill and around blind curves, dodging rubble from landslides or animals that have wandered into the road, leaning on the loud horn as a warning to any who might be tempted to step into his path as well as to friends and other drivers that they see along the way.

The captain pointed out the gun that our driver was carrying, a common sight in Guatemala. Apparently in the past some tourists were robbed by banditos in this remote area leading to Pacaya and subsequently security had been increased.

Vendors, many of them small children, position themselves between the lanes of busy traffic, selling newspapers, drinks and snacks and passing them in through open windows as vehicles pass by. A fruit vendor jumps on our bus and makes his way down the aisle, peddling small bags of peeled oranges and tangerines, chunks of pineapple and tasty looking treats that I don't recognize. He has a little bag of sugar to dip the fruit in if a customer has a sweet tooth. A couple of miles down the road, as we slow for traffic he jumps back off to wait for the next bus.

Leaving the southern suburbs, we continued along the *Carratera al Pacifico*, the highway that leads to the Pacific Coast, past the town of Villa Nueva and through the narrow valley between Volcanoes Agua and Pacaya.

Turning east we left the main highway and began our climb up the hills towards Pacaya.

This road is in much poorer condition and I begin to rethink my choice of seats as we near some machinery blocking most of the road. The driver decides that he has room to squeeze past the obstacle and as I glance down the front wheel below my window appears to be inches from the edge of the eroded, rain-soaked road. It must be the angle I'm watching from, I reassure myself. Besides, the driver makes this trip every day, right?

We have chosen the sunset tour of *Volcan Pacaya* in order to view the dramatic eruptions as darkness falls and it crosses my mind that our bus ride back down this treacherous road will be after dark. Well at least I won't be able to see on the way back, I reassure myself.

"Stick! Stick! Taxi! Taxi!" chanted the Guatemalan children from the little town of San Francisco de Sales, as Captain John and I descended the steps from the bus. It was the end of the road and the place where the trail began on our tour to the top of the volcano.

The captain and I couldn't resist buying a couple of hand carved walking sticks that we stumbled upon in a little market in Antigua earlier, but most of the tourists purchased walking sticks from the young entrepreneurs. Many children in Guatemala work to contribute to the family income, often from a very early age. I find it impossible to resist their beautiful bright faces, almond-shaped brown eyes and friendly smiles. I've bought

Spanish newspapers that I cannot read and trinkets that I have no need or room for, simply because I cannot say no.

"Taxi, taxi", the children continued to chant as we began our two hour climb up Pacaya. The taxis were actually horses - short, tough, sure-footed creatures, led up the volcano by the children, whom I realized must make this climb every day. How hard can it be?

The majority of *touristas* opted for the taxis from the trailhead, or the beginning of the ascent. Others broke down and climbed on after we walked for ten to fifteen minutes and the concept of the two hour hike began to have more meaning.

"Are you sure you don't want to ride up?" urged John, well into the first of the two hours, as he hailed one of the available taxis.

I was already gasping for breath but determined to climb this volcano on my own two feet. Our friends and fellow Canadians from Mario's, Wendy and Graham from the catamaran *"Bravo 2",* had recommended this excursion. They were a few years older than us had made it all the way up. My competitive nature was not going to allow me to give in and take a taxi.

"It's hard work", Wendy had assured us, giggling mischievously, "but well worth the effort."

The higher we climbed the more annoying the constant "taxi, taxi" chants became. I was unable to put together enough words in Spanish to say, "I want to climb up on my own." Actually, I was unable to put together any words at all.

The few remaining climbers, a bunch of backpackers my kids' age, were gaining ground on me. Stopping periodically to catch my breath, with my hot black jeans clinging to my sweat soaked legs, I fumbled for anything dry to clean my fogged-up glasses. Finally I gave up, took them off, and stowed them safely in my backpack.

I only needed to see about four feet in front of my face anyway because with the steep grade of the hill, that is where the ground was. By this time the captain was once again urging me to take the "taxi-taxi" horseback ride the rest of the way up. I shook my head defiantly, having no breath to answer him and the next time that I heard "taxi, taxi" I snarled an impatient "*NO MAS TAXI, TAXI POR FAVOR!*" Nobody bothered me again.

The group ahead of me had reached the first rest point, a lovely spot overlooking *Lago Amatitlan,* nestled in the heavily-forested hills below. Gazing down upon the tranquil scene, high above the clouds in the valleys between the mountains, I had barely stopped to take pictures when the guide motioned me to follow along. He wanted to keep the group together for safety reasons.

I lagged behind the rest of the group on the entire way up Pacaya. Each time I reached a rest stop, the others in the group, who seemed younger and younger as time went on, lurched ahead - leaving me, the matriarch of the group, without my rest period.

Every few minutes, one of them would give in and hail a taxi, renewing my determination to conquer this beast on my own.

About half way up, after the first excruciating hour, the skies opened up in true Guatemalan rainforest style. Others scrambled for rain gear and ponchos but I welcomed the cold rain, which cooled my skin as it soaked through my thick, black jeans.

Angry bolts of lightning flashed in the distance. Thunder roared and the trails below our feet turned to muddy paths as they wove their way up over rocks, around trees and stumps. Higher and higher we climbed. Everywhere we looked little rivers of rainwater ran downhill faster than we were climbing up.

Part way through the second hour, the group fell into a quiet, reflective - almost meditative state and even in my exhaustion a feeling of peace came over me. In single file we climbed in silence, walkers and riders, slipping and sliding. The air became cooler as we climbed higher and my wet clothes ceased to bring me comfort. Finally reaching the highest point, we were rewarded with a stunning view of the vast, smoldering landscape of the mighty Pacaya.

After our long uphill struggle, we were then faced with a steep downhill climb to a large, bowl-shaped basin below. The taxis were left at the top to await their passengers' return. The grade was too steep and the footing too treacherous for even these sure footed beasts of burden. As the captain and I stopped to catch our breath and take in the scene before us, the rest of the pack scrambled down and across the charred, hostile lava field, drawn towards the glowing spectacle in the distance. The physical agony of the climb was suddenly forgotten as we gazed upon the otherworldly landscape.

We snaked our way across, stepping carefully from peak to peak of the hard, crusty surface. To lose our footing and put a hand down to break the fall would certainly result in injury. Our walking sticks were a godsend as we tested each patch of cooled lava before stepping onto it. We had heard of people accidentally stepping into a soft patch, only to slide into the hot molten lava below.

At one point, the guide circled back to help me navigate a particularly challenging stretch of terrain, holding my arm and showing me the way, step by step. He congratulated me on walking all the way up, holding my arm high in the air in a victory stance, proclaiming "*La chica es muy forte!*" The captain rolled his eyes and I read his mind.

"*No - la chica es muy loco.*"

When we reached the edge of the crater, we were only a few feet from the river of molten lava, glowing in the falling darkness. The more daring members of the group were attempting to roast hot dogs and marshmallows on the ends of their walking sticks, drawing back from the intense heat, snapping photos of their fearless antics. The Mom in me could barely stand to watch them posing precariously near the edge of the crater.

Our wet clothes began to dry instantly from the heat of the lava. We had gone from sweltering in the tropical heat to shivering in our soaking wet clothing after the torrential rain. Now, we were drying out by the fire and getting nice and toasty again.

After snapping some photos and shooting some video footage, I suggested to the captain that we sneak off and get a jump start on the return trip. I knew that the kids would catch us once they started back. We retraced our steps across the lava field and began our climb back up the steep terrain to where the horses had been left.

From there, we would begin the long climb back down the mountain. With darkness falling and the climax behind us the two hour trip down the wet, slippery trails wasn't very appealing.

Another couple caught up with us as we made the steepest climb of the trip, more crawling than walking, stopping once in a while to catch our breath, crouching close to the near-vertical ground in an attempt to keep from tumbling down. A thunder boom jarred us all and the woman just ahead of me screamed out in fright as lightening grazed the top of her head.

We learned later that a horse from another group heading up the volcano behind us had also been hit by lightning. The rider had been unseated as the poor creature plummeted down the side of the hill.

Stopping to catch our breath before we crawled up the last, short stretch to where the horses were waiting, we crouched on the ground and took in the ghostly scene. Above us the mountain top was obscured by thick fog. All we could make out were the shadowy forms of the waiting horses. Below us darkness and fog erased the path we had taken.

The edges of the narrow pathway leading up fell off into the foggy darkness, testing the captain's fear of heights. But before long it was all downhill, which turned out to be just as grueling as the climb up. In the darkness it wasn't easy finding the trail and when we did our shoes disappeared into the boggy mud. We had neglected to bring a flashlight and after I slipped half a dozen times, landing on our boxed lunches in the knapsack on my back, our guide lent me his flashlight.

Once again the members of our group, huddled closer together in the dark than they had been on the way up by the light of day, became increasingly quiet, speaking only to notify those behind of the dangers underfoot.

"Slippery! Big rock! Careful here," echoed voices in the dark, as beams of flashlights pointed out one obstacle after another. By the time we reached the bottom, I was in dire need of a *bano* - first, and a cold *cervesa* - second.

We hobbled up the stairs onto the bus and literally fell into our seats. We were cold and wet and blistered and hungry and thoroughly exhausted. The return bus ride down the steep, slippery road in the dark was the least of our concerns and even the youngsters in the group nodded off on the long ride back to Antigua.

Thankful that we had caught the bus in the Central Square, just a few blocks from our hotel, our legs were wet and numb, our feet raw and blistered. Neither of us had worn anything but crocs or flip-flops for months and our feet had been in wet shoes and socks for most of the day. We didn't feel like we could take one more step.

We have since learned never to assume anything when traveling in Guatemala, such as that a tour might end at the same place it began. To our dismay, the bus stopped on the far side of town, near the bus station and we were forced to limp all the way across town to our hotel.

"I'm starving. Do you want to see how badly squished the sandwiches in my backpack are?" I asked the captain, since we hadn't eaten anything since breakfast.

"Thanks, but no. Sorry, but they didn't look very good when we started out." he replied, so I tossed them into a wastebasket and we picked up some hot pizza before hobbling home. We peeled off our mud encrusted, still wet clothing, devoured the pizza, which was now cold, and fell into a deep sleep.

Our climb to the top of *Vulcan Pacaya* was the most physically challenging experience I have ever endured and one that I will never forget. I honestly don't know if I would do it again, knowing what I know now. Maybe next time I'll take the taxi.

September 2

Our trip to Guatemala City and Antigua has been a great success. We found a new, English model laptop for a great price and had our hard drive replaced in the old laptop, again at an excellent price.

Our much needed break from the confines of the boat and the humidity in the Rio Dulce has come to an end and it is time to return. After our adventurous, but exhausting trip from the Rio, we opted for the $16.00 luxury trip back. A mini-bus would pick us up at our hotel door at 9:00 am, we were told. From there it would take us to the bus station in Guatemala City, where we would catch an air conditioned bus, equipped with a washroom, for the five-hour return trip to the Rio Dulce.

At 10:00 am, the mini-van was still twisting and turning around the streets of Antigua, repeatedly passing the hotel we had just checked out of. It was 11:30 before we arrived in Guatemala City for the 10:00 bus. Our tickets were exchanged for the 11:30 bus, we were ushered on and off we went. The air conditioning was cranked so high that I wore John's coat for most of the ride. I guess the thinking must be to get the bus as cold as possible before nearing the Rio Dulce, where the extreme heat makes a/c almost useless on the bus.

We soon realized that this was no express bus, as we stopped in every little town imaginable along the way. In one town, a large bus part was loaded onto the bus. When we stopped for the normally brief lunch break, the driver, his helper, and several other men crawled under the bus, removed the old part and installed the new one.

Forty-five minutes later we were finally on our way. When we reached Morales, about a half hour from home, the bus stopped and we were all herded off. Every piece of luggage was removed and loaded onto a second bus, along with the passengers before we continued the rest of the way. We had left at 9:00 am and it was 7:00 pm before Marco picked us up from town in the *launcha* and returned us to the marina. Some luxury trip!

We had left the a/c on in the boat in our absence. But due to almost daily power outages, it had stopped and not restarted. The boat was about 100 degrees Fahrenheit inside, a somewhat appropriate welcome back to the Hotter than Hell Rio Dulce! Home, sweet home!

The bus we rode from Fronteras to Guatemala City

Las Torres Guest House in Guatemala City

Waiting outside Las Torres for the taxi to the bus terminal

Guatemala City

We passed this parade as we arrived in Antigua

Guatemalan women selling hand woven fabrics in Antigua

Musicians on a typical Antiguan street

Posada San Sebastian, our hotel in Antigua

The magnificent view from our rooftop garden in Antigua

Looking down on Antigua from the Hill of the Crosses

A young girl in Antigua who sold me a head bandana

John, taking the "taxi taxi"

John and me, soaking wet after our climb up Pacaya

The burning lava on top of Volcano Pacaya

Guatemalan woman selling treats through the open bus windows

An unscheduled stop on the way home from Guatemala City

Chapter 9

Back to the Boat

September 11, 2007

There was major excitement a week ago when it looked like Hurricane Felix was headed this way. We attended our first captain's meeting at the Cayuco Club. Meester Jeem sat perched on a bar stool with a clipboard in his hand. The boaters in attendance were briefed on the details of the 72-hour plan. It would go into effect the next day at noon if the storm was aimed at us.

First thing the next morning, a few hours ahead of schedule, the 72-hour plan went into effect, since the storm seemed to be coming in our direction. The first task was a fuel run using the marina's pontoon boat - filling jugs for those who needed gas or diesel fuel.

Some boats would opt to move away from the marina before the storm and all boaters wanted to be ready to move if they had to. Everyone was starting engines, testing batteries, filling water tanks, and running by dinghy into town to stock up on necessities like groceries, beer, and rum.

Several unattended boats were moved out of the marina and anchored in safe places, in some cases with an armed guard for the duration. The boat beside us was the first to be moved. This was an enormous relief to us. Since it had been tied a mere foot from *Diamond Lil*, it was our biggest concern if we received significant wind.

The next stage of the plan was to strip canvas off the unattended boats at the marina. We all pitched in to help, stowing any loose articles on deck and canvas down below. In a place where just thinking about moving causes one to break a sweat, this was a hot job. The decision of whether to remove canvas was left up to the crew of each attended boat.

We were all asked to confirm whether we planned to stay or go in order that plans to space out the remaining boats could be formed. We are at the far end of the marina, in the most protected spot, but some boats up by the club that receive much more wind decided to leave.

It was Monday night and we carried on with our pot-luck plans. By the time the pot-luck was held at 6:30 pm, Felix had veered south towards the Honduras/Nicaragua border. The 72-hour plan was quickly aborted. We hadn't taken down our canvas, since we were more worried about rain damage than wind. It turned out to be a wise decision.

Boats started returning to their slips the next day and life resumed as normal. We received a little over 24 hours of rain and the water level rose quickly during that time, but the following day dawned clear, sunny, and hot!

September 17
11:50 p.m.

The alarm on my cell phone jolts me awake, signaling
the beginning of my watch. Sliding out quietly from
beside the captain in the dark comfort of our stateroom,
I creep up to the cabin, reach for the VHF radio and hail
Bill on board *Gabriella.*

"*Gabriella, Gabriella.* This is *Diamond Lil.* Over."

"*Diamond Lil* - this is *Gabriella.*"

"Do you have anything to report?" I ask.

"No. All quiet," reports Bill.

"Okay. Get some sleep," I answer. "*Diamond Lil* - out."

Eileen Quinn's catchy tune "Where Have All the Pirates
Gone?" runs through my mind as I shine my bright
spotlight slowly around the anchorage, pausing slightly
on our two buddy boats, making sure no banditos lurk
nearby.

The night is alive with the sound of fish jumping and
several gar pike pause in the beam of my light. Huge
birds catch my light for a fraction of a second as they
skim the water. Upon closer inspection I realize that
these are not birds, but bats - huge bats with big, fat
bodies and wide wing spans.

I am thankful to have drawn the 12:00 am to 2:00 am
pirate watch, as I savor the stillness of the night. Had I
lay sleeping in my cozy bunk, I would not have

witnessed this magical display. I feel privileged to be here in this nocturnal paradise.

Years ago, long before we bought *Diamond Lil* and set off on our travels, John read "Pirates on the Rio Dulce," an article in the August 2002 issue of PassageMaker magazine, written by Peter Swanson and Ron Wooldridge. The story about Dan Caruso, from Palmetto, Florida and his two teenage nephews being surprised by three pirates as they lay peacefully at anchor way up the *Ensada Los Lagartos*, in Guatemala, seemed a lifetime away to us at the time. Over the years, we fantasized about venturing to this exotic land. Over and over, we would thumb through our magazines until we found the "Pirate" issue.

Lago Izabal is the largest body of fresh water in Guatemala at 30 miles long by 15 miles wide. It lies at 26 feet above sea level and has a maximum depth of 59 feet. Cruisers can choose from remote locations such as the anchorages of *Ensenada Los Lagartos* and *Ensenada Balandra (El Refugio),* or more popular tourist attractions around the lake.

"Have you taken your boat up to Lago Izabal to anchor?" I asked several of the boaters at Mario's Marina.

"Are you kidding?" was the usual reply. Most had not made the trip, having heard too many stories of dinghies and outboard motors being stolen. It just wasn't worth the risk. A few brave souls had made the trip but not without taking precautions. Their advice was very similar to that outlined in the "Tips for

Staying Safe" portion of the PassageMaker article we had read, many years ago.

We were out for our morning walk yesterday, when Gail, one of girls I walk with regularly, casually mentioned that her family was heading out for *Ensenada De Izabal* early the next morning. Another boat in the marina, *OK FINE*, was going too, as a buddy boat.

"There is safety in numbers," she said. "Do you and John want to come along?"

I couldn't wait to get back to the boat to see if I could talk John into going. He hesitated at first, but I can be relentless and here we are!

At the top of the list of the safety tips is the advice to travel with one or more buddy boats. *Diamond Lil*, the odd man out, a powerboat in a sea of sailing vessels, has joined *Gabriella* and *OK FINE* on a cruise from Mario's Marina on the Rio Dulce in Guatemala to the notorious *Ensenada Los Lagartos* at the far end of beautiful Lago Izabal.

Joan and Art Schucks on *OK FINE*, a 42-foot Irwin cutter ketch, have been liveaboards since 1989 when they left their home in Oregon and sailed from Charleston to begin a new life in the Caribbean.

After running a successful charter business for many years, they returned to the United States and endured the heartbreak of losing their first vessel, *That's It,* to Hurricane Katrina in Biloxi Bay. They bounced back, purchased *OK FINE*, and have been sailing the western Caribbean since 2002.

Although considerably older than us, they are among the bravest and most adventurous of cruisers on the Rio. Joan, who is a breast cancer survivor, requires an hour's treatment each morning. Her devoted husband sets this time aside each day without fail. They have overcome amazing odds to be among the bandito watchers.

When I asked what made them decide to head out into the lake despite all the horror stories, Art replied that, like us, they had questioned many experienced boaters on the Rio and decided that the spectacular scenery made mandatory night watches worth the effort.

Aboard *Gabriella*, a 47-foot Voyage catamaran, are three generations of the Gordon family. Ted, Gail, and their fifteen-year-old son, Trevor, have taken two years from their life in Tavernier, Florida to sail to the South Pacific. As they wait out hurricane season here in Guatemala, they are joined by Ted's father, Bill.

Bill is also a cancer survivor. Instead of giving up on life when he lost a leg to the disease, he embraced life, working in the Florida Keys as a sailing and diving instructor for the handicapped. Bill cheerfully straps on his artificial leg in the dark of the night and takes his share of the watches.

When I asked the Gordon family what made them decide to head out into the lake, all agreed that the beauty of the area was worth the extra effort. They were thankful to have us join them (many hands making for lighter work), but had been prepared to stand watches themselves if necessary in order to visit the area.

We have agreed to maintain radio contact 24/7 on a previously decided station, to take turns exploring the area by dinghy, so that someone is always with the boats, and to take our hand held radio with us when out exploring, to maintain contact.

We "fly our dinghies," that is pull them up out of the water at night and lock them to the boat. We have a local cell phone, fully-charged with a new pay-as-you-go card installed. We are posting bandito watches all night long; eight adults, dividing the night up into two hour segments. Each person is to communicate at the end of his/her watch with the next person coming on watch by VHF radio.

Using bright spotlights, we scan the anchorage and the area around the boats, keeping our eyes and ears open for anything unusual. Apparently one of the most common times for an attack is in the pouring rain, when the sound can drown out that of an approaching vessel. As the night air cools, I am able to turn off our fan and can thereby pick up sounds outside easier. My air horn is within reach, as noise is apparently a big deterrent to would-be banditos.

When we do leave the boat we lock the door and all the windows and stow valuables well out of sight. Most crimes are apparently crimes of opportunity, with thieves wanting to get in and out as quickly and quietly as possible. We feel a little paranoid as we tuck our laptops away, but losing them is our worst nightmare.

We have already had to replace one laptop and one hard drive in Guatemala, not a shopping experience we care to endure again. I leave the TV out in plain sight as our sacrificial lamb. We can't get a signal down here anyway and it would be easier to replace than a computer.

September 17

Well worth the efforts we have taken to make this trip, we woke this morning to the unmistakable roar of howler monkeys, coming at us in stereo from the trees surrounding our anchorage.

I sprang from bed like a kid on Christmas morning and rushed out to view the spectacular scenery. Towering over us at 9,892 feet to the north are the majestic mountains of *Sierra de Santa Cruz.* To the south, the peaks of *the Sierra de Las Minas* lay shrouded in mist and cloud. The mountains are carpeted with patchwork quilts in countless shades of green, suggesting order in this endless sea of jungle. Smoky fires dot the landscape, the only sign of life as far as the eye can see.

To the west, at the headlands of the lake, is the *Reserva Bocas del Polochic,* one of the richest wetland habitats in Guatemala. This remote lowland rainforest is home to more than 220 different species of birds, including toucans, parakeets, and parrots. An early morning dinghy expedition led us deep into the steamy jungle, creeping quietly along the undisturbed mirror-still rivers.

September 18

After two nights anchored in the infamous *Ensenada Los Lagartos*, we set off with our buddies to explore the lake and spent the night anchored in what is known as the most protected anchorage on the lake, a remote bay known as *El Refugio*. We have yet to spot another pleasure craft on the lake. It's a little eerie.

September 19

Parting ways with *Gabriella,* as she headed back to Mario's Marina, we continued on with *OK FINE* to Denny's Beach, a popular resort on the southeast shore of the lake. It is slow season now and we were the only boats, in fact the only guests at the resort.

The Beach Resort Hotel has a wide variety of accommodations, including cute little private cabins tucked up among the tropical plants on the steep hills, with a lovely view of the lake, dormitory style lodging for backpackers, and even campsites. Backpackers make up a huge segment of the tourists in Guatemala. There are free mooring balls for visiting boats and even a dock that is free to tie up to.

There are free kayaks available to use and wakeboarding in the busy season. There are beautiful walking trails up through the jungle as well as along the beach. Many tours are available to various other tourist destinations around the lake. There is a choice of two horseback riding tours. We took the shorter, four-hour trip, which included a stop to swim in a refreshing mountain stream with a series of waterfalls.

We chatted with Roberto Lujan who has been managing the place with his wife, Laura Morelra, for only a few months. He mentioned some of the additional features of the resort, including the armed guard who keeps an eye on visiting boats and a first aid center for use not only by resort guests but anyone on the lake in need of assistance who finds themselves closer to Denny's than to a hospital.

They have a stock of anti-venom required for some of the poisonous snakes in the area, which is important because time is of the essence when bitten by some of the nasty ones. We even enjoyed free internet from our anchorage just off the beach.

Denny's doesn't keep the horses used for the tours on site, they simply notify local *caballeros* when someone books a tour and horses are brought in from the area. They can provide eight horses fairly quickly and 18 more with a little more notice.

We thoroughly enjoyed our ride through the little town, the pastureland with a wide variety of cattle, horses, and pigs and then up the mountain. We cooled off in the stream and frolicked under the waterfall before heading back down. I glanced upstream at one point, and then quickly looked away. Our tour guide was perched upon the wet rocks, butt-naked.

It is such a shame that more cruisers don't take their boats to Denny's Beach and we took a handful of business cards with us when we left, vowing to be back, hopefully with more boats next time.

Oct. 6, 2007

Thrilled to be untied from our dock at Mario's, we set
out to explore the mysterious anchorage at the far end
of the *Golfete*. My excitement turned to disappointment
after we spent the first night anchored in a little spot
called Texan Bay.

I longed to sleep with the hatch open, feel the breeze
and hear the wildlife, but what we ended up hearing
was the noisy Honda generator that the boat next to us
kept on his deck. He ran it all night and it literally kept
us awake. It was a beautiful, cool night, so why he felt
the need for it, I don't know.

So, we pulled up the anchor and went back to the scenic
spot where we spent our very first night in Guatemala.
We dropped the hook beside *Cayo Grande*, the jungle
paradise that I remembered fondly from that night.

With my binoculars, I spotted a large toucan up in the
trees. I felt renewed and refreshed as we swung gently
through the dark green water.

I scrubbed the hull from bow to stern and the back deck
and transom, ridding us of scores of spider nests full of
un-hatched eggs and little baby spiders. I love to do this
hot work when we are anchored. I can work in my
bathing suit without a marina full of people watching
me. And I can jump in the water every time I get hot.

Before heading back to the marina, we planned a photo-
op for *Diamond Lil* along the gorge. I need photos for the

article I am currently writing for PassageMaker
magazine.

The plan was for me to follow in the dinghy and film the
boat from the water, so we could get shots of her
underway. I was having a great time, photographing
Diamond Lil in the exotic setting, from every possible
angle, until I stalled the outboard engine.

"Come closer," I instinctively called to John, who was
driving the big boat.

"Are you kidding?" he yelled over the sound of her twin
engines. "I can't get that close to you."

I could see his arms flailing about his sides as he
watched me drift further away. I could see his mouth
opening and closing and imagine some of the words he
was using. I was too far away by now to hear. It was
probably just as well, I thought. He had wanted me to
take the hand-held radio with me but I insisted that our
chatter would spoil the authenticity of the video and left
it behind.

He managed to turn *Diamond Lil* around and get close
enough to me to yell, when suddenly flames began
shooting out of the motor. My first thought, which came
in a flash, was to jump into the river. My second
thought, which followed a split second later, was that I
had both my still camera and my video camera around
my neck. I could not jump.

"Take your shirt off, wet it in the river, and put it over the engine," he yelled. Obediently, I ripped off my shirt, sending all the buttons popping into the river and dumped in it the water. By then, the fire had fizzled out. My favorite shirt was ruined. Some guys will do anything to get you to take your shirt off!

Later, Captain Fix-It discovered that a gas line had come undone and quickly repaired it, but the episode sure livened up my photo session. The photos of the "Little Trawler that Could," our *Diamond Lil*, against the background of the canopy of jungle cascading down the cliffs, was worth the aggravation.

When we arrived back at Mario's, the sailboat which is normally docked a mere foot from us was just pulling out. YES! Not only do we have a much nicer view but it was a perfect time to have the hull waxed, since it is sparkling clean. We have Marco's boys waxing the boat for us and she is gleaming! The labor rates are very low here, in fact it is only $3.00 per hour to have this done. The work is too hot for me to do, now that we're back in our slip.

Two of my three walking buddies are gone for now. Sarah has gone by boat to Belize. Carol has gone by bus to Mexico for three weeks. So, it is just Gail and me and she is leaving for the Honduras Bay Islands en route to Australia in a few days.

This morning we walked to Esmeralda and I took some pencil crayons, paper, paints, paintbrushes, a puzzle, and some gum to the kids in the village. These kids draw some amazing pictures, for their age. It's probably because they don't spend any time sitting in front of a television. They are very poor and appreciate anything we can give them.

I also took a very cool wind-up flashlight with a radio in it that our friend Mikey gave us when we were in Canada. I gave it to a young boy who was about three years old. The look he had on his face, as he worked the buttons and figured out how to make the light and music work, was priceless!

Gail and Ted brought medical supplies to distribute among the clinics in the villages, as do many of the cruisers down here.

Tonight, we are heading over to *Gabriella* for dinner, before the crew sets sail for the South Pacific and then we will walk over to the Cayuco Club for karaoke night. John has always despised karaoke, until now. It's a lot of fun here, where we know everyone.

"Maybe I'll sing one night," I tell him.

"Go ahead. I'll leave if you do."

"John, that's mean, that's a terrible thing to say."

"Rusty around the edges," he said. It was a line from his bio, when we met online, years ago. He uses it as a disclaimer for his behavior, whenever he feels like it.

I baked muffins and brownies this morning and have

been feeding them to the boys who are out waxing the boat. I'll make some cheesy scalloped potatoes to take to the pot-luck dinner tonight. Life is good!

November 26

Many times over the summer I thought that if I didn't escape this steamy, sweaty place I'd go crazy. Now that we are about to leave, I realize what a wonderful experience it has been to spend these past five months living in this little jungle paradise.

Stepping off the bus in Fronteras after the long ride from Guatemala City is like stepping onto a movie set. It's noisy, hot, dusty, sticky, stinky, and bursting with color. Swarms of bees buzz around the heaps of ripening fruit along the sides of the road. Pedestrians walk along the far too narrow stretch of roadway between 18-wheelers, cattle trucks, and buses. Motorcycles and scooters wind through vehicles and pedestrians alike.

Walking through Fronteras takes total focus. The streets are broken and uneven, riddled with obstacles for the *tourista* who is not paying attention. Wheeling our three rolling suitcases and lugging more bags, a laptop, a backpack, and cameras through this kaleidoscope of life feels like adventure travel. But no - it's just us, heading back to life as we know it on the boat.

"Are you going to the islands for the winter?" we heard over and over these last couple of months.

"What islands?" I asked the first time. I had no idea what they were talking about.

"The Honduras Bay Islands," they said.

"There are three main islands – Utila, Roatan, and Guanaja, as well as a few smaller ones. Most of us head there after hurricane season. It's popular for diving because of the clear water and the world's second longest reef."

We watched our neighbors, Jim and Jeanie on *Oasis II,* cast off from the dock on their way out the Rio a couple of days ago and we won't be far behind. Like most boaters, they had timed their departure to correspond with high tide because of the shallow bar that must be crossed heading from Livingston Bay out into the Bay of Honduras.

It can be a major obstacle to boats with deeper drafts and there are always "bar crossing" horror stories going around. Jeanie called me today to ask me to look up the marine weather on the internet for her. She reported that they had a very bumpy bar crossing, dragging all the way.

With our 3 ½ foot draft it isn't an issue for us. We will wait here and keep an eye on the weather this week. With respect to leaving the Rio, we are the envy of every boater here at the marina, not having to plan our departure to correspond with the high tide.

The marine forecast calls for winds from the east 20-25 knots for the next couple of days and then east and

northeast 10-15 knots so we will wait here patiently.
Memories of big, open water and wind are fresh enough
that I don't care to poke our nose out there until
conditions are perfect. After five months, what are
another few days?

We have enjoyed a couple of days of slightly cooler
weather, but for the most part it has been HOT. Today,
it rained off and on and heavy at times. I wondered how
Jim and Jeanie were making out. So, after a long
afternoon nap, I called to see how they were faring out
in their anchorage at *Cabo Tres Puntas*, after six
months at the dock. We tease Jeanie and call her a
Princess because she always has long, painted nails and
doesn't care for the heat. You can usually find several
air conditioners running in her boat.

A few miles can make all the difference in weather here.
Only 20-30 miles to the east, on the "outside" she
reported that the weather had been hot, breezy and
pleasant and that they were enjoying clear Caribbean
water in a flat calm anchorage. We hope to catch up to
them on our way to the Honduras Bay Islands.

John installed the new macerator pump that we picked
up in Florida and fixed our wash-down pump. We can
wash the boat, one last time, in fresh water, before
leaving.

We downloaded marine charts and cruising guide
excerpts from Jim and Jeanie and have been busy doing
the million and one things that need to be done before
casting off from shore and living on the hook for who

knows how long. We have been stocking up on provisions as we head into unknown territory, not knowing what we'll find in the Bay Islands.

It's exciting heading out to sea, going exploring once again, but it's also a little intimidating. We've adapted to this quirky little place on the Rio Dulce and become quite at home. The Call of the Ocean is always there though.

I can almost hear the waves from here.

Meester Jeem leading the captain's meeting at the Cayuco Club

Making a fuel run , part of the hurricane preparedness plan

Walking through Esmerelda with Sara, Gail and Carol

Sara and I become good friends and traveling companions

Our two buddy boats, anchored in Ensada Los Lagartos, Guatemala

We met aboard *OK FINE* to discuss our security plan

Islands of floating water hyacinths drifted through our anchorage

Ted and Gail from *Gabriella*

Our buddy boats – *OK FINE* and *Gabriella*

The remote town of El Estor

Captain Fix-It, checking our power cords

Diamond Lil, anchored at Denny's Beach, Lago Izabal

My mount for our horseback riding tour at Denny's Beach

John and our tour guide

Cooling off in the waterfall before we rode the horses home

Our tour guide chose a private spot upstream – not private enough!

Chapter 10
Honduras Bay Islands
Utila

December 1, 2007

The longer you stay in one place, the more difficult it is
to move on. After calling Mario's Marina in Rio Dulce,
Guatemala home for five months, we finally untied the
dock lines. Today, we begin our next adventure.

It seems fitting to me, as we drop anchor in front of the
town of Fronteras, that we spend our last night here.
What a different perspective I have now, after our five
months in the Rio. On that first dark and stormy night,
Fronteras was overwhelmingly offensive to me. Now it
is familiar and not at all threatening.

As excited as I am to be on our way, it is a bittersweet
farewell. My love and hate relationship with the Rio is
in the love phase, as we stroll the lively street in search
of a few last minute provisions.

December 2

From the hectic waterfront of Fronteras, we traveled a
short 15 miles, through *El Golfete,* and dropped our
anchor in Texan Bay. Once again, I am reminded of my
childhood treks from home to our family cottage.
Birdsong and the odd plopping sound of a fish jumping
from the water breaks the silence. Every so often sounds
of friendly chatter and laughter waft across the

Bay, from the marina in the distance.

December 3

Sneaking quietly out of the anchorage at Texan Bay, we made the 9 ½-mile trip up the river. We anchored in front of the town of Livingston and by 10:00 am we were in town to meet Raul, the immigration officer. We can't say enough about the efficiency of Raul, who has prepared our exit papers based on information we emailed him from Mario's Marina a few days ago. Clearing out of Guatemala was a breeze and cost only 640 *quetzals*, a little less than $100.00 U.S.

Leaving the Rio Dulce, we traveled another 14 miles due east, across the Amatique Bay. We dropped anchor at Cabo Tres Puntas, which translates to Cape Three Points.

It's a narrow strip of land, thirty miles long and only about five miles wide, at the northeast tip of Guatemala. The *cabo*, or cape, juts out into the Gulf of Honduras, forming a natural boundary between Amatique Bay to the west and Omoa Bay to the east.

It will be our last night in Guatemala. When we round the point in the morning, we'll be entering Honduran waters.

"It feels great to be anchored again after six months of being tied to shore," I announce to John. "It's so exciting to be somewhere new."

December 4

"It's nice to be anchored again, is it?" teased the captain, as we rose before dawn. After a long and mostly sleepless night my euphoria had disappeared. The chop and roll of the anchorage made me seasick as soon as I got up. How quickly I forget, I reminded myself.

"Look at this, honey," I said to John. I had noticed a small lump on one breast during the night.

"Is it sore, or itchy?" he asked. "It looks a little red."

"More sore than itchy," I said.

"Hopefully it's nothing and will go away, but we'll keep an eye on it," said hubby.

"Can we leave at first light?" I pleaded, changing the subject.

"We can try," said the captain. "If you think you can get the anchor up in this chop."

I looked out at the bow, watching it rise and fall in the choppy sea, dreading the task of pulling up the anchor.

"I'm pretty sure that once we round the point, we'll find calmer water," reassured hubby. And he was right.

Once we rounded the tip of land we had anchored behind, the wind was in our favor, and we enjoyed a comfortable trip to our next anchorage at Puerto Escondido, which had been highly recommended by several of our fellow cruisers.

Puerto Escondido means hidden harbor, and it most certainly was. We made a 45 degree turn and headed south through a narrow opening into the circular shaped bay. It was completely protected from every direction. Tucked into the northwestern coast of Honduras, where the Ulua River runs into the Caribbean Sea, it is considered an archeological site, with history dating from between 1600 BC and 450 AD.

The captain circles the bay slowly, as usual, looking for the perfect spot to anchor. He runs his fingers absent-mindedly through his beard. Finally, after much thought, he nods at me and snuggles up to the west coast of the basin.

The late day sun casts a dark shadow of the western peak against the brightly-lit summit of the eastern tip of the basin. We are surrounded by massive cliffs, covered in a thick jungle of palms, towering above our heads. We are in exotic Honduras - the lone boat in a private tropical paradise.

December 5

Mother Ocean delivered a perfect day for our last leg of the trip to Utila. Calm seas beckoned us across the Gulf of Honduras. I am overwhelmed as I realize that we are once again cruising on the Caribbean Sea in our little trawler from Canada. What a dream come true.

A pod of dolphins, frolicking in the crystal clear sea, sent me scurrying for my video camera. I film our yellow quarantine flag and our Honduran courtesy flag, flying

high on our flag pole, as we glide across the ice-smooth
sea.

By 2:00 pm we were anchored in a broad bay in front of
the island of Utila. It is the smallest of the three main
Honduras Bay Islands, the furthest west and therefore
the closest to Guatemala, which is why we decided to
stop here first. We have logged only 166 miles from
Fronteras in the Rio Dulce to Utila. It's remarkable to
travel such a short distance and end up in such different
surroundings.

The island is only about 14 kilometers long by three
kilometers wide. Roughly two-thirds of that area is
covered by mangroves and water. Utila is also the
closest island to the mainland of Honduras, about 35
kilometers away.

When I first stepped ashore I was reminded of Bimini,
in the Bahamas. To John it seemed like Hopetown, also
in the Bahamas. It is wonderful to be back in the
islands. Everything is better - the water, the sand, the
walking, the food, the music, even the grocery stores.
After spending two weeks searching for hard to find
items in Fronteras, we discovered that the grocery
stores in Utila have a much better selection of food.

The official currency of Honduras is the *lempira*, at an
exchange rate of about 19 *lempiras* to one U.S. dollar,
which has us scratching our heads once again as we
price and pay for things. Utila is the least expensive of
the Honduras Bay Islands and a popular destination for
low budget travelers, which seemed like another good

reason to stop here first.

The official language of Honduras is Spanish but here in the islands the main language heard is English, with a definite island accent. Spanish is also widely spoken.

The Bay Islands are on the southern fringes of the world's second largest barrier reef and are Honduras' main tourist attraction. The main draw in Utila is the array of inexpensive dive programs offered. People travel from all over the world to become certified to dive here. Many return time and time again. It is also very popular with the young, backpacker crowd.

The main road is lined with dive schools. Boatload after boatload of eager divers come and go, day in and day out, and even at night sometimes.

For many divers, swimming with a whale shark is the dream of a lifetime. The whale shark is most definitely a shark; a slow moving, filter-feeding shark. The largest specimen on record was 12.65 meters or 41.5 feet long and weighed more than 21.5 tonnes, or 47,000 pounds.

Despite its size, the whale shark presents little danger to divers other than accidental injuries from unintentional blows from its tail fin. It is known as the least fearsome of the shark species and has therefore become a major attraction for divers.

The whale shark, or Rhincodon Typus, inhabits all tropical and warm-temperate seas. But Utila tops the list of worldwide locations where divers have the opportunity to get up close and personal with this gentle giant of the sea.

Typical coloring of a whale shark is dark grey with random white lines and spots on the body. The fish is believed to live between 70 to 100 years and reaches sexual maturity after about 30 years. It swims at a slow speed of about three miles, or five kilometers, per hour.

Utila is also nicknamed the party headquarters of the Western Caribbean. The young crowd dives by day and parties at night. Loud music carries over the water and goes on until about 4:00 a.m. Just as the throbbing music shuts down, the sound of early risers, starting generators on nearby boats, wakes us. It's a lively place, and a nice change to hear the action from our snug little home in the bay.

December 7

"I noticed a fairly modern looking medical center on the island," said the captain this morning, as we enjoyed breakfast at a little outdoor café. He had on a grey Guatemala t-shirt, with a photo of the Rio Dulce on the front and on his head, wears a Canadian ball cap. He has finally relented and trimmed his beard short and neat, shaving years off his life - appearance wise, that is.

After breakfast, we strolled towards the west end of the island. There was construction underway and we had to detour along a sandy path that ran alongside a deep trench, running for quite a distance along the island.

We waited at the medical clinic in line with several teenagers who were having the requisite pre-dive physicals and a couple of locals who looked like they might not survive the day. An elderly lady sat slouched on the bench outside, coughing and hacking.

Dr. John McVay, known simply as Dr. John, is the only doctor on the island. There is no air-conditioned waiting room with stacks of glossy magazines or a cold water dispenser in this clinic. The waiting area was no more than a gathering of benches outside, most of them in the full sun.

Shifting position on the bench outside the building to try to position myself in the ever moving shade, I wondered whether it was wiser to get closer to the old woman with the nasty sounding cough or just sit in the blistering sun. The captain grumbled and shifted and moaned and groaned. Knowing what a poor waiter he is, I conjured up an errand and sent him off.

Finally, my turn came and I saw the nurse - a burly Australian fellow wearing the top part of a medical uniform, cut-off jeans, and bare feet. He led me into a storeroom which also served as an examination room. He asked me a few questions, filled out some forms and told me to return at 1:30 pm to see the doctor. He asked me to bring my husband, since there was no woman on staff. Because I was having a breast exam, I was required to have a witness with me.

The captain and I returned a couple of hours later and once again waited our turn outside on the bench in the sun. The teenagers were back for their results. The old woman was still there and still coughing.

There was a new patient as well - a rough-looking young guy. If I had to guess I would have said he was strung out on some kind of drug. He lay flat out on the bench, smoking a cigarette with his eyes closed, muttering and complaining about the wait.

My name was called and the captain and I were led into a crowded storeroom with an examination table sitting in the middle of it. I was given a gown to change into. When the doctor came in it was all I could do not to laugh out loud.

His long hair was tied back in a ponytail under a crocheted Rasta-type hat. He had a long, thick beard, a heavy mustache and dark, thick-rimmed glasses. He wore beach-type shorts and a short sleeved cotton shirt with a tropical pattern. I would have taken him for a beach-bum or low budget tourist if I'd passed him on the street.

As my mother used to say - "Don't judge the book by the cover."

Dr. John was very professional as he shared with us the good news and the bad news. The good news was the lump was definitely not cancer; it was in fact something he saw and treated regularly on the island. The lump was a cyst that had become infected.

The bad news was that he would have to drain the cyst, in addition to prescribing antibiotics because in the 'petri-dish' like environment of the islands infections spread like wildfire - much quicker than in our Canadian climate.

I could see the color drain from hubby's face as Dr. John described the simple surgery and began un-wrapping needles and scalpels. The captain hates the sight of blood and we were warned that there would be some, perhaps quite a bit, in addition to the cheese-like matter and pus that would need to be drained.

"Since you have to be here", I told the captain, "You might as well take some pictures".

I asked Doctor John if he minded and he assured us that he was the most photographed person on the island and we were free to take as many pictures as we wished.

In fact, he told us, since there wasn't often much news on the island, any kind of bloody, gory medical emergency would result in the local TV news reporters following the patients to the clinic with their news cameras. They would be allowed to film, unless the patient objected.

"May I use the washroom before you start?" I asked.

The nurse led me around the corner to a small *bano*. As I hiked up my gown and sat on the toilet, the seat skidded off and landed on the floor. It wasn't attached. There I was, ready for my surgery, picking up a toilet seat from the floor of a third world *bano*.

Back on the table in the middle of the storeroom/examination room, as the good doctor cut and squeezed and scraped, John got into his role as photographer. It took his mind off his initial revulsion at the thought of this odd character slicing into his favorite part of my body.

The wound was packed with gauze soaked in iodine. I was bandaged up, given a ten day course of antibiotics, and instructed to return tomorrow to have the packing removed.

Tomorrow is Saturday and the clinic is closed, but the nurse told us to come in at 3:00 pm and the doctor would make a special trip in for us. He told us that the doctor had spent all of last Sunday here, also when the clinic was closed. He had revived the old woman we had seen waiting out on the bench earlier after a particularly bad spell. She was a tough old girl, he told us. Not to worry – she'd be fine.

The bill for the office visit, procedure, supplies, and antibiotics came to 1,825 *lempiras*, which sounds staggering, but it's only $96.00 U.S.

Imagine the cost of such a procedure in the States or Canada. There would have been a referral to a specialist, a lengthy series of tests, and a long wait for the procedure itself. It was simple here. We walked out of the clinic about an hour later and the old woman and sorry looking young man were still there.

December 8

As directed, we returned to the clinic today at 3:00 pm and had the packing removed and the wound dressed - free of charge this time. I was given instructions on cleaning and caring for it and came away with deep respect for this strange man who tends the sick and writes a column called Dr. John McVay's Utila Rap.

We read his column in the local publication, The Bay Islands Voice (www.bayislandsvoice.com). He has found his niche and is a hero to the people on the island.

His poems are more like collections of one line rules to live by or scattered thoughts.

Freedom is the lack of fear

An old life still has a new day

Thoughts are you.

Depression is free of charge.

We are thankful and relieved that the lump was only a cyst. We will continue on to the island of Roatan in a couple of days. It is a much larger island, with numerous anchorages and a much safer place to be with the boat.

After waiting for three days for the immigration officer to show up here on Utila, we asked Dr. John if we knew where we could find him. Dr. John told us that he has been gone for a month and nobody knows whether or not he is coming back. Check in on the island of Roatan, he told us.

So, in the morning we'll up-anchor and make the 40-mile trip, due east to Roatan.

Fuelling up at Ram Marine, before leaving the Rio

Heading east, leaving the *Golfete*

Heading through the challenging cut to Puerto Escondido

Afternoon sun casting shadows on the hills of Puerto Escondido

This sailing *cayuco* passed us in the bay in front of Utila

John, enjoying delicious Honduran coffee in Utila

Waiting for my surgical procedure at the Health Clinic in Utila

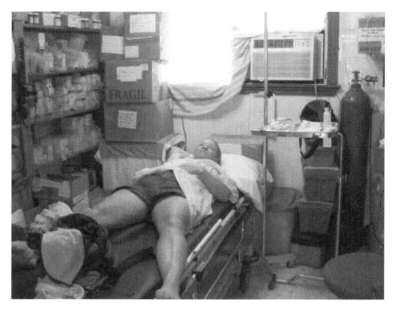

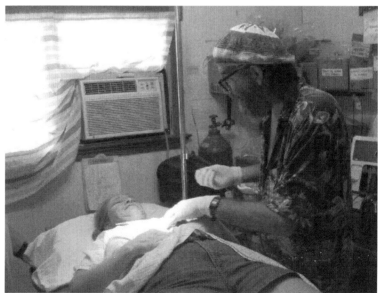

Dr. John – the only doctor on the island and a local hero

Chapter 11

Roatan, Honduras Bay Islands

Dec 12, 2007

Roatan is the largest, best-known, and most-visited of the three main Honduras Bay Islands. It stretches almost 40 kilometers long but is only about three kilometers wide, at the widest point. It is the most popular of the islands for cruisers. This is because of the many anchorages around the island as well as smaller islands and cays to explore nearby.

The inlets and bays on the southern shore of the island that once attracted European pirates and loggers now attract scuba-divers. Along the northern shore is a combination of beaches and cliffs, with fewer anchorages.

It is a diver's paradise, with the reef just a few hundred meters from the north shore and coral formations very close to the beach along the southern shore. The islands are made up of a mountain range that disappears into the sea a little further west, with the tops forming the central hills that add to the charm of the island.

Although the immigration office is in the town of Coxen Hole, the capital of the Islands, it is not the most desirable of anchorages. Our friends at Mario's Marina have suggested that we anchor in French Harbour. From there, they promise, we can catch an inexpensive taxi ($2.50 for two people) into Coxen Hole, to check in with immigration.

As the sun sets to the west, I truly feel like we are in paradise. We are anchored in the vast anchorage referred to as French's Cay Harbour. The water is turquoise blue and crystal clear. The bay is flat and calm, protected to the south by a long reef.

Several sailboats and a catamaran share this Caribbean paradise with us. As the sun sets, the green drains from the peaks to our west and turns to charcoal as the sky behind glows bright orange. As the sky fades to black, we are treated to a show of sparkling lights - in clusters along the shore and here and there, scattered high, up in the mountains.

December 13

My time in our picturesque anchorage came to an abrupt end, this time due to our outboard motor. We made it into town with no problem and enjoyed browsing the quaint streets. Unfortunately the trip back to the boat, after the motor quit, was much longer. The anchorage seemed much larger than before, as we paddled furiously, against the current back to *Diamond Lil.*

"We'll have to move her into the inner harbor, at least until we get the engine fixed," said John. "We can't possibly stay out here with no outboard.

"Oh, no," I wailed, for I had seen the inner harbor, when we parked the dinghy there to go ashore. But it was no use; the captain had made up his mind. So, we up-anchored from paradise and moved *Diamond Lil* a couple of short miles into the creepiest place I could imagine.

Much of the town surrounds the harbor, which seems to be used for waste disposal - resulting in plastic bottles, diapers, and assorted debris floating by and lapping up along the sides of the boat.

However, we are within rowing distance of the Roatan Yacht Club. Several of our old neighbors from Mario's Marina are here on their boats. Jim and Jeanie, from *Oasis 1* and Tom, *from Oasis 2,* are here. Our boats were docked three in a row back in the Rio – what a small world it is!

December 14

We are patiently waiting for an outboard mechanic to show up to look at our motor. He was due yesterday at 5:30 pm and when we finally called him, he said he would come *manana.* We have learned that *manana* does not necessarily mean tomorrow. It does usually mean - not today!

Until our motor is repaired, we must stay within rowing distance of the dinghy dock at the marina. I can't wait until the outboard is fixed so that we can return to the beautiful anchorage just outside the inner harbor.

We were offered a ride to Coxen Hole yesterday by a helpful boater at the yacht club, which we gladly accepted. Jamie is a large black man, over six feet tall and quite heavy set. His sixty-foot dive boat, *Divers at Play*, looks enormous here at the dock. Usually Jamie can be found sitting bare-chested outside the boat, or on the back deck, with a big, fat cigar in his mouth. It isn't normally burning, but he chews on it constantly.

He is a nice guy, but man can he talk. Luckily, I rode in the back seat. John, sitting up front, was not as lucky. The stories went on and on. If he's done everything he told us about, he must be much, much older than he looks.

"Uh-huh. Yeah. Uh-huh," I heard John trying to sound interested. I was content to watch the sights and tune them both out.

Jamie dropped us off right in front of the immigration office. He was still talking when we closed the door and waved good-bye. We peered into a tiny, dark office and were summoned in and had our passports stamped.

There is no charge to enter the country with the boat and no charge for us to stay for 90 days. We purchased a Honduran cell phone for $30.00, to keep in touch with family.

I gave up on the $3.00 per hour internet at the marina, after spending an hour uploading four photos and one video clip. Instead, I walked into town to the internet café, which charges 40 *lempiras* an hour, (about $2.00) and their internet is much faster.

December 15

Despite it being a mostly rainy week, the day of the French Harbour Christmas Festival dawned sunny and bright. With the streets of the downtown area closed to cars, we wandered from the yacht club towards the festival with Jim and Jeanie from *Oasis 1*. Originally from Dallas, Texas, they were our boat-neighbors at Mario's Marina and we had spent a lot of time together.

Jim was a bit of an old hippy. He always wore a cotton skull-cap tied over his head, usually one printed in a tropical pattern. He wore wire-rimmed glasses over his brown eyes and sported a thick mustache. He was a happy soul, always smiling, with laugh lines around his eyes to show for it.

Jeanie was fairly tall, with blue eyes and a cheerful, round-cheeked face. Unlike most women in the Rio, who clipped their hair short, she wore her blonde hair long and straight. I called her Princess Jeanie, because she wore her fingernails long, painted in bright shades of red and pink, with toes to match.

We were joined by another couple we knew from Rio Dulce, Sharon and Joe from *Rose of Sharon*. Sharon was quite a character. When she introduced herself at our first Spanish class, she had everyone in the room laughing.

She was a large woman, with short, blonde hair, who spoke with a lisp. She made a joke of it though. She told a hilarious story about trying to ask a question in the grocery store in Fronteras with the combination of her poor Spanish and lisp.

Sharon has written scores of magazine articles for a boating publication called Tattletales. Jeanie lent me a bag full of them and I am inspired and slightly in awe of her.

The evening air was balmy, as we joined the crowds heading downtown to watch the parade and witness the lighting of the tree.

The town looked much more appealing in the fading light. As darkness fell, the familiar sight of Christmas lights, strung on palms instead of pines, and reflecting in the water rather than on snow, added to the charm. Impressive light displays, although beautiful, seemed out of place amongst the signs of poverty. But then, everyone seemed happy and content – so who am I to judge?

We passed up several roadside selections of local dinner offerings and opted instead for dinner at the highly recommended Gio's restaurant. We had read about Gio's in our cruising guides.

For almost two decades Giovanni Silvestri Ferez and his wife, Rosa, have been delighting islanders and international visitors alike with their own unique blend of Honduran, Caribbean and Italian cuisine.

Giovanni Silvestri Ferez describes his business as a family tradition born of the marriage of his father, Dino Silvestri, of Italian origin, to his mother, Olga Ferez, a native of La Ceiba, Honduras. His signature dish, King Crab, was a family tradition. Over the years, his own version of the dish earned it the title as one of the 30

Wonders of Honduras and the first wonder in the culinary category.

Over the years, Gio's loyal customers' preferences have helped to create some of the items on the menu. The "Eldon's Special" was a dish created for frequent customer Eldon Hyde, who favored a combination of crab, lobster, and shrimp.

"Charly Big Fish," was a dish inspired by good friend Charly Frissel, who preferred a large, hot dish of grilled shellfish and vegetables.

These specials looked delicious but were a little pricey for our cruisers' budgets. Everyone at our table ordered the grouper, cooked in various ways, except Sharon. She went Texan on us and ordered beef. We dined under the stars, entertained by a fireworks display out over the sea.

Satiated, we rejoined the festival and strolled at a leisurely pace back to the marina and headed for our respective boats.

December 20

The captain and I took advantage of another sunny day and made the $3.00 taxi trip down to Coxen Hole, the capital of the island, to buy each other a few Christmas gifts. This in no way resembles Christmas shopping as we have ever known it. It reminded me of shopping in Bimini, Bahamas.

John and I split up and I made my way around town, in and out of shop after shop, looking for suitable gifts for

John. It wasn't easy. Because there wasn't a cruise ship in the harbor that day, most of the vendors who cater to tourists were not there, as they had been on our first visit. The gifts I had seen for John, when we were together and had come back for, were no longer there.

I was the only gringo in sight on this non-cruise ship day, and found the shopkeepers more than eager to make a sale. I quickly learned to ask for things rather than just look for them. Items aren't easily visible or even necessarily displayed, like they are in stores in Canada.

I asked as best I could for the items I was looking for, in Spanish. Once I was understood, more often than not, the shop-keeper would motion for me to wait and rush out of the shop and down the street, shouting to the other shop-keepers along the little alleyway.

Typically, within a minute, he or she would return, with the item in hand. Often, after I handed over my *lempiras* to pay for the item, a similar routine would occur. Off the shop-keeper would go, cash in hand, leaving me there waiting. I soon learned to keep lots of small bills handy. Nobody has change on this island. They joke that you could starve to death with a 500 *lempira* bill in your hand. That's the largest form of currency – only about $25.00. Yet, nobody has change for this bill.

After circling the block a few times, I found most of the things I was looking for and enjoyed speaking to many helpful people, about half the time in Spanish and half the time in English.

The closest thing to Christmas wrapping paper I found was something with red roses on it. I remembered seeing some in the grocery store in French Harbour. It is sold by the single sheet at a cost of ten *lempiras* a sheet, which is about 50 cents. It is quite different from the mega-roll packages of paper for sale back home. Christmas seems much simpler here and not nearly as hectic.

December 21

Finally – the outboard motor has been repaired and we are free to return to the idyllic anchorage by French's Cay. I snapped several shots of another golden sunset and a shot of our lobsters, sizzling and turning ruby red on the barbeque.

December 22

My euphoria was short-lived, however, as we headed into town today for supplies. Our motor had a relapse, coughing and sputtering, and then finally dying altogether. So, up came the anchor and back we went, to the quagmire of an anchorage close to town. John ordered a couple of parts from the U.S., which will be shipped to us after Christmas.

We have both had enough of this slimy, stinky anchorage. The carcass of a dead pig floated up and bumped up against Jim and Jeanie's boat yesterday, or at least the remains of one. Now I know where the pig's head that I saw hanging in town came from.

Of course, I had not been able to resist taking a photo of it.

"What is it for?" I asked the islander, who was watching me and chuckling.
.

"Someone will buy it," he said. "To eat - it's a delicacy."

Later, back at the marina, we stood and talked to Tom, from *Oasis II.*

"The outboard motor is the Achilles heel of the cruiser," said our boat-neighbor, Tom. He is right. *Diamond Lil* is our house, she goes where we go. The dinghy is like the family car – we need it to get back and forth from our house to shore. We need it to explore. Many places down here are water access only so we just plain need it.

We had the fuel pump and carburetor rebuilt last week. John repaired a ground wire, sanded and cleaned all the grounds, replaced questionable looking connections, drained the gas and the carburetor, and added new gas and oil. Finally, he ordered a coil and module from Florida, which won't be shipped to us until after Christmas.

We surely didn't come to Roatan to sit in this carcass-filled inner harbor. Dinghy or not, we're off to explore.

"Let's go to Old Port Royal," I suggested. "There are remnants of four forts to explore. After a short, 16-mile cruise eastward along the island, we anchored up tight to shore and rowed in to walk around a little cay. It seemed like we were in a very remote spot when we anchored. But boat after boat whizzed by *Diamond Lil.* It was a little unsettling.

"There is a canal through the mangroves, up there," said John. "That's why there is so much boat traffic. It's the main waterway to the island of St. Helene, which is only separated from Roatan by a small canal."

Once darkness fell, it became a remote spot. We couldn't see a single light, in any direction, except a red one on top of a communications tower. There were no houses, no other boats - only us.

December 23

I had heard that there was a place in Port Royal, which is different than Old Port Royal, where you could get free internet access from your boat. Apparently it came from a house on shore, whose owners like to help cruisers. I was on a mission to find it but as we cruised towards the west, parallel to the shore, the captain grew tired of me pointing to every structure and yelling "Maybe that's it."

"Forget it," said John. "I read that we can get internet access in Jonesville, at a place called Hole in the Wall. Continuing east, for only nine miles, we found Jonesville Bight and made our way into the harbor.

I've been in Internet HELL since we got to Roatan. The only place I've been able to connect was at the internet café in French Harbour. And even there, the speed was slow. We were on a quest to find internet, somewhere!

Once in Jonesville Bight, we anchored but had no idea where Hole in the Wall was. We noticed an internet signal coming from Woodside Marina but couldn't connect. Our radio crackled to life.

"*Diamond Lil, Diamond Lil*, this is *Oasis II. Over.*" It was Tom.

"*Oasis II*, this is *Diamond Lil*," I replied.

"Jim and Jeanie just called me. They just passed you in a small boat. They are over at Hole in the Wall with some friends for the barbeque and they want you to join them."

The Hole in the Wall is famous for its Sunday all you can eat beef and lobster barbeque.

"That sounds great," I said. "We'll try to start the outboard, but it's been giving us a lot of grief, lately."

"They'll pick you up from Hole in the Wall," said Tom. "They offer the pick-up service because the place is water accessible only."

We dropped the dinghy, hoisted the motor onto it, only to have it not start. Not to worry! A call on the VHF radio to Hole in the Wall had a boat over to pick us up in two minutes flat. I dragged along my laptop, in case

Hole in the Wall had internet access but found when we arrived that their system was down.

The people were very friendly; we were made to feel like a part of the crowd from the moment we stepped onto the slightly crooked dock.

Hanging from the ceiling and covering the walls was a collection of autographed t-shirts and baseball caps from all over the world. Graffiti covered every available surface - the tables, the chairs, and even the washroom walls. We were encouraged to leave literary evidence of our visit.

A basket of big, fat cigars were free for the taking and before long it seemed like every guy in the place, and even one woman, were puffing on them. John was quick to join in, and I snapped a photo of him with the beast in his mouth.

The meal was a man-sized feast, with tender beef, succulent lobster, heaping pots of mashed potatoes, home-made bread and salads. The view was equally enjoyable.

Another jungle canopy covered the hills across the bight. To the south, just past the reef, lies the deep blue Caribbean Sea and beyond that, barely visible, are the peaks of the mountains on the Honduras mainland.

Before long, we were introduced to Mr. Larry, the owner of Woodside Marina, in front of which we are anchored. He was a salty looking character. He looked to be in his late sixties, with thinning grey hair, freckled skin, and bright blue eyes. He too came here by boat, he told us. He too is from Canada - British Columbia in his case. He loved the island, so he scrapped his trawler and made it into a house. He's been here since 1994, he tells us, and bought his property in 1995.

As he told his story, Mr. Larry spoke quite a bit with his hands and as he did, it was impossible not to notice that he was missing a couple of fingers on his left hand. One of the remaining fingers looked like it had almost been lost, as well.

"Come and meet Mr. Bob and his sidekicks," said Larry.

In the middle of the bar was an odd, rectangular shaped table, about chest height, with three tall, wooden bar stools around it. Lounging in the three wooden bar stools were three unique looking characters. I noticed right away that all three were barefoot.

Mr. Bob, proprietor of Hole in the Wall, was a big guy, sort of a Santa Claus look-alike. He had snow white hair, with bushy sideburns, a mustache and big snow-white beard to match. He wore jean shorts, a Hole in the Wall sleeveless white t-shirt, a brown ball cap and eyeglasses, which hung on straps around his neck. He shook my hand vigorously, as Mr. Larry introduced us.

"Hello. How are you?" I said, as Mr. Bob took my hand in his.

"Right here," said Mr. Bob.

"Melanie. I have a daughter named Melanie," said Mr. Bob, with a twinkle in his bright, blue eyes. "She's my favorite, you know."

Mr. Bob spoke slowly and carefully, with a calm deep voice.

"Your house is beautiful," I said. I couldn't help but notice the impressive stone structure, which looked to be built into the side of the mountain.

"Thanks," said Mr. Bob. "It took a whole year to cut all the stone out of the hill and another whole year to build it."

Next we were introduced to Harry and Dwayne. Mr. Larry pointed to a couple of sailboats, docked around the side of the bar.

"That's where Harry and Dwayne live," said Mr. Larry.

Harry was fairly short. His hair was salt and pepper, with his sideburns, moustache and beard more grey than his hair. He had a small, round face and spoke with a high, almost squeaky voice. He wore beige shorts and a black, short-sleeved cotton shirt.

Dwayne wasn't much taller than Harry. He had a thick head of brown hair and big brown eyes. His mouth was just a small slit between a massive brown beard and a thick, brown mustache. His nose was wide and flat, like he'd spent some time in the boxing ring. He wore a short-sleeved cotton shirt, with a tropical flowered pattern printed on it.

"Dwayne must have been a cowboy in a previous life," I joked to Mr. Larry, as he walked over to the bar. His legs were severely bowed.

"Blacksmith," said Mr. Larry. "He was a blacksmith."

"Ah. That explains it," I said.

Mr. Larry offered to connect us to his internet server once he got back to his place. Finally, my prayers have been answered. For the first time since leaving Mario's Marina in Guatemala, almost a month ago, I will be able sit back in the comfort of my own boat and enjoy the internet!

We have a dilemma on our hands. We can either stay here, anchored in front of Woodside Marina in Jonesville, where we have internet. Or, we can head back to Fantasy Island, in French Harbour, with some of our friends, for a Christmas turkey dinner.

"I can make dinner on the boat," said John. The internet won out. Jonesville it is for Christmas.

December 25

"Merry Christmas", I said to a local fellow we passed as we enjoyed a Christmas afternoon stroll through the town of Jonesville. "How are you?"

"Right here" he replied and I wondered if he'd been into the holiday rum.

I sat down on an upturned *panga*, one of several piled by the side of the road. Relaxing in the shade of an old oak tree, I watched the sea, which was as dead calm as I'd ever seen it. Not a ripple stirred the surface, as I called my family to wish them a Merry Christmas.

This is the third year in a row I've been away from home at Christmas. The first year we spent with John's parents in Port Charlotte, Florida – a short detour from our Great Circle Loop Route. The next year, we spent

Christmas at the Bimini Blue Water Resort, in the Bahamas.

And now, here we are, spending Christmas on the gorgeous Caribbean island of Roatan.

I thought back to one of the very first on-line conversations John and I had – before we had even met.

It was a cold, February day in Canada. I asked him how he was and he answered, "Pretty good. But I'd rather be on a slow boat south."

A man of few words, I always say about my guy. But when he decides to do something, there is no stopping him.

December 29

Mr. Larry has offered to run John over to see an old islander in the next town who has outboard parts for sale. If we could find the coil we need for our outboard motor, it would be a miracle. Once the outboard is fully functional again we will be free to explore the area.

There is canal access to several communities, located in different bights along the south coast, enabling boats to travel back and forth without going "outside" into the deeper water.

These bights offer protection from the northeasters that haunted us back in the Florida Keys and Bahamas the last couple of winters. We thought that by coming this far south we would escape them, but apparently not.

Best to stick to the south coast, we have been told, for now. As the weather improves in the months ahead we can explore the north coast, which doesn't have the same protected anchorages. Then, we can also travel to the town of West End, the touristy area at the west end of the island.

Yesterday, we took the dinghy along this shallow stretch of the waterway that we have been reading about, which is protected from the reef just offshore, allowing small boats to travel between several bights and towns.

A low footbridge along the route prevents bigger boats from using it. We were able to enjoy a close up view of the communities along the coast. We tied up the dinghy at a dock and walked through the pleasant town of Oak Ridge, browsing through a couple of grocery stores and stopping for lunch at a diner along a dusty little stretch of road.

What a surprise - chicken, rice and beans, fried plantain and lettuce with the usual Thousand Island dressing. Most of the local places have no menus, you just eat whatever they have that day, usually chicken with rice, beans and lettuce with Thousand Island dressing and fried plantain.

December 30

I'm always compelled to climb to the top of large hills or mountains for a view of the scenery far below. This morning, I talked John into joining me on my climb from the end of the little dirt road near Mr. Larry's house. It was a little cloudy when we set out. Once the sun came out it was a hot climb, but worth it for the spectacular view in every direction.

We arrived back at the boat at the same time as a local fisherman who had lobster, king crab, and grouper for sale. We ended up with 21 small lobster tails for $22.00. It looks like I have a reprieve from chicken with rice and beans for a few days!

"Mr. Larry, I have a question," I said the next time we ran into him at Hole in the Wall.

"Twice now, I've asked someone how they are and they answer "Right here." What's with that?"

"Ah. That's an island phrase," said Mr. Larry. "It's island speak for "Everything is alright here.""

I guess the old fellow we passed on Christmas morning hadn't been into the rum after all.

"Mr. Larry, I have another question. Where do people go around here to celebrate New Year's Eve?" I asked, as the big night drew closer.

"HUH!" huffed Mr. Larry. "We usually go over to the Hole, but not late at night. We go over in the evening and celebrate early. I haven't seen midnight in years."

Wonderful, I thought to myself.

"Well, the young people, where do they go?"

"OH, they go to West End. There are all kinds of parties to choose from there."

"But the captain says the weather is too unpredictable this time of year to take the boat to West End," I explained.

"Well, it can be," said Mr. Larry. "Rent a little room at Chili's. It's right across from Sundowners. That's where people go for happy hour. The rooms are cheap and right on the beach. My guests always stay there when they go to West End. You'll find plenty of New Year's Eve action there."

I pleaded my case to the boss.

"Nah, we don't want to do that," he insisted. "It will be fun here – you'll see. We can go to West End when the weather gets better. Don't worry – we have lots of time."

"But, honey. There is nobody here but crusty old sailors and bachelors. There aren't any women."

"Sure there are. There were girls down at the bar."

"They work there, John. I'm going to sit around with all you old geezers smoking those stinky cigars and talking about pumps and motors all night, while all the fun is happening down in West End. You're so stubborn."

And so, much like Christmas, it looks like New Year's Eve will find us here in the booming metropolis of Jonesville.

Last year, we spent New Year's Eve in Green Turtle Bay, Abacos, Bahamas. The year before that we had been in the Florida Keys with our friends from Canada, Deb and John. The year before that we had flown to Puerto Vallarta. We wondered last year, where this New Year's Eve would find us.

"We back the clock up six hours," joked Randy French, an old sailor we had met at the Hole in the Wall. "We officially celebrate then, not at midnight. That way, by eight o'clock, we can be in bed."

He too, had come here by boat, years ago. He had retired from a career repairing electronics. He only stood about as tall as me and I'm sure weighed much less than me. He had snow white hair, rail-thin legs and arms and wobbled pretty badly when he walked. His voice was distinctive and his laugh quite contagious.

Thankfully, I was spared an all-male New Year's Eve. We met Don and Yvonne, a couple who had also come here by boat. They first visited the island in 1989. Then, in November of 2004, they left their home in Fells Point, Massachusetts, and like us, took a slow boat south.

"We took our time," said Don. "It took us nine months. We didn't actually get here till July of 05."

Don was not much taller than me. He had thick, greying hair and a huge handlebar mustache. Above his dark brown eyes were dark, bushy eyebrows.

Miss Yvonne wore her grey hair beautifully curled. She was dressed in a classier outfit than one might expect for a rickety wooden bar with rickety wooden tables and chairs. She wore a matching scarf, thrown in a stylish manner over her shoulder, and had put on a fresh coat of lipstick. I felt like a boat bum compared to Miss Yvonne.

She was a rose among a bunch of thorns, as our little group of boaters, dreamers, and castaways began the countdown to midnight, or in our case, 6:00 pm. As the clock struck 6:00, we kissed and cheered and clinked glasses. And, like old Randy said, by 8:00 pm we were fast asleep.

January 7, 2008

The first time we arrived in French Harbour, I cringed at the thought of taking a boat slip. We had only been living "on the hook" for a week or two at the time and after five months at Mario's I felt like I'd never want to tie to another dock as long as I lived. It's funny how time changes your perspective.

We returned to French Harbour a few days ago and I was shocked to hear myself suggest to the captain that perhaps we should take a slip for a day. The parts for our outboard motor, originally due at the FedEx depot on the island on Friday, were now due Monday.

We haggled and bartered with the folks at the French Harbour Yacht Club and the next thing I knew we had a low, one-time only, never-again weekly rate of $80.00 which includes power, water, internet, cable, use of the pool, and marina grounds.

It is a nice change to step off the boat and go for a walk whenever we want. It is also nice to put the kettle on in the morning without starting the generator first. It is nice to have ice, compliments of our icemaker and to watch television on the boat for the first time in almost a year.

On our first night here we watched the New Hampshire U.S. Presidential debate and it brought back fond memories of my father and how he loved to watch those kinds of shows. He'd warn us all at dinner - we could watch with him if we wanted to but we had to be quiet as he sat there and made notes, underlining them with a ruler. The ruler was important, he would tell us. Only a Neanderthal would underline without a ruler.

The only news stations we receive here in French Harbour, other than CNN, are from California and Colorado, but any news is fun to watch when you haven't seen it for a while.

In true Central American fashion, our FedEx delivery has slipped steadily from Friday to Monday and then most recently to Wednesday at 6:00 pm. Since the office closes at 5:00 pm, the earliest we will receive our part is Thursday. We've learned to be patient.

Neither of the two bank machines in town were working and the lineup in the bank was so long that John gave up and returned to the marina. Of all the places we have visited, this is the worst for getting cash and very few places accept VISA. He had lunch, returned a little later, and still waited an hour and a half in the line-up, part of it outside the bank in the sun, to finally reach the teller.

The culture is very different when it comes to buying and paying for things here. Even people who work for the government are not always paid on time but have to wait patiently for their cheques. Perhaps this is why it is quite often acceptable to pay later for things on the island.

The owner of the Roatan Yacht Club was murdered last year, at the same time as a marina owner in La Ceiba, a city on the mainland close to here. Apparently there were quite a few "hits" at the time. Drugs, the rumors claim. The marina has been in a state of flux for the past several months, with the restaurant and bar temporarily closed.

A new owner is due to arrive next week and slowly there are signs of progress. The hotel is beginning to receive guests. The restaurant has started to serve breakfast this week, and apparently will be serving other meals soon. Unfortunately, rates are increasing, which is why our haggling for this week's price probably won't work in the future.

The grounds are beautiful with a very long, steep climb from the marina down at the bottom of the hill up to both the clubhouse and the road into town.

The internet works except for when the power goes out, which is almost every day. Within a few minutes of the power shutting off, the generator starts up and life goes on.

We hope to get out and enjoy a little sight-seeing on the island during the next few days because the boat is safe and sound here at the dock. We are never totally comfortable leaving the boat at anchor to head out for any length of time. As much as living on a boat buys a certain amount of freedom, there are times when the opposite is true. We rarely go out at night because we don't like to leave the boat alone.

However, as the captain reminds me if I complain about anything, I could be sitting in a cubicle wearing pantyhose or shoveling snow and fighting traffic. Washing our sheets in a bucket on the boat, along with all our laundry, since there are NO Laundromats on this end of the island, isn't that bad when you think about it!

January 9

Surprise! Surprise! FedEx delivered our package unexpectedly here at the marina - two days before we thought we would have to taxi down to pick it up. The captain had the parts installed in the motor in no time flat and we were off to spend the afternoon at Fantasy Island, with our friends Jim and Jeanie.

The management at Fantasy Island welcomes cruisers to use the facilities, free of charge. I was impressed with the resort and was in and out of the pool and the ocean, back and forth, snorkeling, swimming, sunning, and of course filming! There was an amazing variety of creatures wandering around as well as some eye candy for the guys!

The captain found postcards and took me to look at them. He probably didn't spot the 50% off women's clothing sign, but I did. I have added a tank top, bright and colorful with an underwater fish scene, for only $11.20, to my wardrobe. The quality of postcards leaves much to be desired here, but I picked up a few. Now, if only there was a post office in this town!

We are watching the weather closely because the captain has finally agreed to venture down to West End, the happening part of the island. There are free mooring balls to tie up to, but only for use in suitable weather. This means light wind coming from the east or southeast, which is what we see forecast for the next several days.

Taking advantage of the internet access here at the French Harbour Yacht Club, I have been working with a copy editor from PassageMaker magazine. My next article will appear in the Web Exclusive Articles section of their online edition. The article should be live in a few days. It only pays about half what a magazine article would, but it's still good exposure.

I have another article appearing in the March/April issue of Living Aboard magazine, so I am off to a good start this year, with four articles set to be published, so far.

January 12

Our trip to West End was well worth the wait for good weather. We have been blessed with two days of flat calm water, light breeze, and sunny skies. This settled weather becomes more common as the winter progresses, but for now we are cherishing each day that we have here. I know that whenever we leave, it will be too soon!

Yesterday, we enjoyed snorkeling on the reef just beyond where the boat is moored. The warm, crystal clear water is perfect for drifting along in the light current, watching the colorful reef fish. I followed a big black grouper for a while and watched a school of beautiful purple fish, which I haven't identified yet. I can't wait to get back out there today!

We had breakfast at one of many restaurants that offer free internet when you order a meal. I'm trying to upload a couple of short videos that I made but there is far too much to do here to spend much time on the computer.

January 16

Life is slow here in West End. The speed of the internet is equally slow. The people at Rudy's Restaurant are very patient and accommodating. Breakfast yesterday took about half an hour to be served. The time to upload two short videos to my website took about four times that.

Finally I packed up my laptop and wandered down the sandy roadway along the shoreline. I stood waiting patiently at the end of Ronnie's dock, knowing that soon the captain would look up from the boat and see me. Eventually he did and came in the dinghy to ferry me and my laptop back to the boat.

I realized a while later that I accidentally uploaded one video twice and missed the second one altogether. I guess breakfast at Denny's Restaurant is on the agenda again tomorrow.

John and I enjoyed a taste of West End nightlife, on Saturday. The choices are endless. Open air bars beckon with reggaeton and soca music. From one to the next we wandered, take-out cups in hand. Before long, we were on the dance floor at Fosters, shaking our booties to the throbbing music.

As a result, yesterday was a lazy day. We swam out to the reef, only to discover that it was a lot further than it looked. John returned for the dinghy and as he was about half way back, I found myself surrounded by jellyfish. They were everywhere. The water was so thick with them, it seemed impossible to avoid them.

I tried to stay calm and swim through the hundreds of floating purple sacs. That was bad enough, but then I spotted a barracuda following me. Thinking that he was attracted by the sun reflecting off my underwater camera, I swam with my arm above the water, looking back periodically only to see him still following me.

I called for John to come for me in the dinghy but he
was still swimming back to the boat. I must have looked
like a crazy woman, out there flailing and screaming.
Within seconds, the man from the boat moored next to
us jumped into his dinghy and came to my rescue.

 With super-human strength, I launched from the water
into the stranger's dinghy. It looked like I frightened
him, but I quickly explained what had happened and
thanked him profusely. John was still trying to unlock
our dinghy from the boat, as I was dropped off safe and
sound on our swim platform. Next time we will
definitely take the dinghy over to the reef when we go
snorkeling.

January 19

Time has slipped by in West End and we can hardly
believe that we've been here for nine days already. We
had only planned to spend a few days here. Mother
Nature finally dealt me a stacked hand. The front that
was forecast to arrive a few days ago was weak and
uneventful and we were able to stay on our mooring
ball.

Our water tank is empty and we have a prescription to
pick up in French Harbour. Otherwise, we probably
wouldn't leave at all. I cannot remember the last time
we stayed in a place as gorgeous as this. I feel like I've
been reading about this town in novels all my life. I
didn't really believe such a fairy-tale, beachfront
paradise existed.

We finally broke down, hauled some laundry to shore,

and dropped it off at a laundry service directly beside the Denny's Restaurant, where we get free internet access with breakfast. It was a great plan, a perfect example of multi-tasking.

However, when we asked what time the laundry would be done we were told, "No luz," which directly translates means no lights, but here in Roatan it means no power, or as they say here – no current. The sound of generators running in town has become so common that at times now we fail to notice it. Alas, there will be no laundry done today, nor could we get internet access at Denny's. However, the kitchen was open. I feasted on a breakfast burrito, with salsa and sour cream. John went for the stack of pancakes with bacon.

Just as we were trying to decide whether to recover our dirty laundry and head back to French Harbour, the "luz" came back on and we're back to Plan A. I will catch up on the website and email messages while the laundry is washed and dried.

We last did laundry on Nov 29th, at Mario's Marina. That was approximately three weeks ago. Since then, I have been washing it by hand and hanging it out to dry on the boat, which isn't a big deal, except for the small amount of water we carry (80 gallons). We need a lot of showers when we are snorkeling every day, which doesn't leave a lot of water to do laundry.

Eighty gallons may sound like a lot to landlubbers but it really isn't. Normally 80 gallons lasts us about a week.

We buy five-gallon jugs of water for drinking, coffee, tea, and cooking.

I was thrilled this morning to receive an email from my sister-in-law and best friend, Donna. She and her sister, Kathy, have booked a flight to Roatan on February 8th. They are staying at the Henry Morgan Resort on West Bay.

After we heard the news, we went down to snoop around and get some photos to send to the girls. I can't wait to have some friendly faces from home and some women to talk to! John can't wait either, to drop me off to talk to some women and give him a break.

The batteries in my camera died, so a couple of days later I decided to head down to Henry Morgan's and try again to get some pictures. John dropped me off in the dinghy, looking forward to a few quiet hours alone on the boat. I would take my photos, and then walk back. We arranged a place to meet in West End.

It was quite a long walk up and down huge hills. When I reached the top of an enormous peak, I came upon the entrance to a zip-line ride. It takes people from treetop to treetop way up high in the rainforest. Kathy mentioned perhaps trying the zip-line when they were here. I was excited because John wouldn't dream of it, with his fear of heights.

A group was just heading out from the first tower. I filmed them as they whizzed through the air, high above the jungle. Then, I decided it would be fun to follow them and film their entire ride.

"Si.Si," said the operator, as I asked him if the trail led to the anchorage down below. It would be perfect. I'd exit from the trail more or less directly behind where we had *Diamond Lil* anchored.

So, I set off down the trail, stopping to film the zip-line riders from down below, as they flew through the jungle canopy. It didn't look like anyone had used the trail for a long time, in fact I lost it a couple of times and stumbled about in the jungle, a little lost.

Life is strange and in the middle of the jungle, I ran into a couple from Mississauga, Ontario. They were a little lost too, so we joined forces and finally found our way out.

However, when we hopped a little fence and strolled through a more manicured, park-like area, we were stopped by a security guard. He asked for our ticket – in Spanish. We had no tickets because we'd snuck, quite innocently, into the park from the back of it.

We tried to explain in our best Spanish but he wasn't impressed and led us directly to the park entrance, which for us, was the exit. I passed some amazing caves on my walk back along the beach to where *Diamond Lil* was anchored.

John finally noticed me standing in the sand on shore behind the boat. He gave me HELL for leaving the road and taking a short-cut through the jungle. Some of the

best adventures are unplanned. And I made a cool
video.

January 29

All good things must come to an end. I wished we could
just stay in West End, as we up-anchored bright and
early this morning. We rounded the end of the island
and headed due east towards French Harbour, fishing
along the way, for what John calls "real fish."

I pull an endless stream of small snappers and grunts
and trunkfish from the water below our swim platform
but John is unimpressed. He wants something for his
next centerfold shot, one of the monsters that hang out
in the deep water just off the reef.

It's called fishing however, not catching, and we came
up empty handed. We pulled into the last available slip
at the Roatan Yacht Club after our short 17-mile cruise
and were greeted by a Canadian couple from Vancouver,
BC on their 2002 Bayliner.

"We have your book," the woman called out from the
cockpit of her boat. She was referring to the latest issue
of PassageMaker magazine, of which they had a copy.
Go figure. We hadn't seen the new issue yet and here, in
the least likely of places, we ran into someone who had
one. We were thrilled to borrow their copy and accepted
an invitation to their boat for a cocktail. I heard Captain
John cursing under his breath as the woman insisted we
pose for a picture in front of their boat.

"You'll just have to get used to living in the spotlight, honey," I told him once we were back in our own boat.

"I've made you famous." Of all the photos I submit with my articles, the editors always seem to choose the ones of him. I tease him and sing the lyrics to "Baby is a Centerfold". He is not impressed.

January 30

We filled our water tank, hosed down the boat, and pulled out of our slip this morning. I am thrilled to anchor in the outer harbor beside Fantasy Island. All day long, boats full of divers pass us, en route to their dive sites.

"Hi Lil" they call out to me, as I wave to them from where I stand on my swim platform, fishing. I've learned after 2 ½ years that it's easier just to answer to Lil.

Sound carries across the water and we can hear what they say about us. "ONTARIO!" one man shouts.

"Wow, they're smart," another comments. I feel pretty darned smart, living here for six months, while these poor suckers will be packed onto a plane after only a lousy week. How well we remember the days when we were the tourists, drooling with envy as we passed the boaters who were living our dream.

Every few hours, a small blue sea-plane taxis through the anchorage, turning beside our boat to take off into the wind. The view of the island from above in this open roofed little plane must be amazing. I think the pilot is getting to know me, the crazy Canadian woman who always scrambles out to take pictures as he takes off because each day he comes closer and closer.

February 7

We had only planned to spend a couple of days in French Harbour, to do a little re-provisioning before heading back to Jonesville. The stores here carry a much better selection of groceries.

However, by the time the wind let up, a full week had passed and we needed to re-provision again. Finally, today, the wind died down and we were up and away by 7:00 am. We were anchored in Jonesville by 8:00 a.m.

The anchorage fills up on Sundays, with boaters planning to enjoy the Hole in the Wall all you can eat lobster and roast beef barbeque. I wanted to get here early to snag the prime spot in front of Woodside Marina, where the internet signal is the strongest. It was a fine plan, as we settled in and watched four other boats pull in after us, including Jim and Jeanie on *Oasis I.*

John went out in the dinghy to show them the channel into the anchorage, this being their first time here on their own boat. We went over to shore and chatted with Mr. Larry about his trip to the Mosquito Coast of Honduras and watched a slide show he had put together.

As I climbed the metal, circular stairway to his front door, I was reminded that he built his house from parts from the trawler he came to the island on before he scuttled her.

"Mr. Larry – what is that strange looking structure out in the middle of the bay? The bottom looks like a boat, but on top, it's more like a house."

We had heard music coming from the strange looking place last time we were here.

"That's the Float N Sip," said Mr. Larry, making a face.

"I have a friend – a guy named Brian. He lives on his boat - up in Guanaja. That, over there, was his old sailboat. He sold it and the man who bought it turned it into a floating bar. Actually, it's also the local whorehouse. They blast their music till all hours of the bloody morning. I can't sleep."

I called the Hole in the Wall on the VHF radio to find out what time the barbeque started. I was told that with the big crowd expected this week, the barbeque would begin at 2:00 pm versus the usual 3:00 pm.

We ate lightly all day and feasted on lobster, roast beef, mashed potatoes, beans, coleslaw, and home-made bread.

Tourists are ferried over from Jonesville by water taxi to the Hole in the Wall. Here we always find an interesting mix of down islanders - people who live towards the busier west end of the island, tourists - the ones wearing the wrist bands, boaters - who arrive by dinghy or skiff, and locals. Some of these locals are native to the island, but most are gringos, the ones who arrived by boat years ago and never left.

Reunited with several of the people that we met here last time, we feel like a real part of the gang. A boater from the table next to us, who met John in town earlier today, comes over to shake my hand and chat for a while. The lobster shells are thrown into the water beside the dock and we all watch the schools of snappers fight for them.

In one of the washrooms there is a wall-to-wall display of paperback books for exchange. Most guests have chosen one or two but Jeanie tells us how a roach climbed out from behind the one she pulled out of the shelf, so I pass. Back at Mario's we learned to put any used books we acquired into the microwave long enough to kill any bugs waiting to hatch between the pages.

Here we are again, hanging out in Jonesville, the place we come for internet among other things. Each time we visit, we hear a few new stories, meet a few new interesting characters, discover a few new appealing trails or roadways, and notice a few supplies hidden on the back of a shelf in some odd little store.

We find out where to buy bottom paint. We find out which town to go to for beer, for Jonesville is a dry town. We learn where and on which day to buy fresh vegetables. Again, there are virtually none in this town. We discover where to buy purified ice, the kind you can put in your drink and not end up having to run to the head all day.

The town is not high on conveniences, but we don't mind. Slowly we settle into the life. It's the best part for me - taking our time to feel the pace of life here, to get to know people and to have them call out, "Welcome back," as we drop anchor.

A local musician named Bobby Reiman entertained the crowd at Hole in the Wall today. Originally from Chicago, he has lived on the island for several years and writes songs about life here. One such song is called the Roatan Song. The chorus moves me, as I marvel at the way the late afternoon sun, falling on the jungle across the bight, brings it alive with brilliant shades of green and yellow.

Light the breeze blows in the morning, stiff the breeze blows at night
Bright is the sun when it's rising, the full moon sets at first light
Low the tide runs in the winter, high the tide runs in the spring
fish like to bite when it's rising, and a sand fly will bite anything
And it's so fine to be free, and livin' down here so close to the sea
Some call it third world vicinity, I call it being content as can be
Green coconut has sweet water, the dry coconut makes the oil
Coconut chip starts the fire, you can smell that fish tea as it boils
Chata cake tastes good on Sunday, Johnny cake tastes good with tea
Tapado tastes good with some dumplin', and a conch tastes best fresh from the sea

And it's so fine to be free and living down here so
close to the sea
Some call it third world vicinity, I call it bein'
content as can be
Hurricane watch in September, the northers will
be blowin' soon
Early sunsets in December, and the mangoes are
droppin' in June
Carnival week in LaCeiba, and out to the beach
Good Friday
The school children march on the quince, and
they dress in their best Christmas day
And it's so fine to be free and living down here so
close to the sea
Some call it third world vicinity, I call it bein'
content as can be
A critical time it is coming, a lot more people
live here than before
There's been a lot of changes so unbecoming a
beautiful place like this one here
Divers love it for diving, and fishermen love it
for fish,
But an anchor can break it to pieces, so help the
reef help maintain how we live
And it's so fine to be free and living down here so
close to the sea
Some call it third world vicinity, I call it bein'
content as can be

February 18

"That's it - their plane. The time is about right," I
announced, as I strained to hold the binoculars still
against the movement of the boat.

"Here. Let me see," said John, taking a turn trying to
catch the name of the airline on the side of the plane.

"We're on our way to West End, to meet Donna and Kathy. And – there's their plane," I said, narrating as I filmed the Air Canada jet come to a stop on the short runway that Roatan is known for.

I was afraid that Mother Nature was going to trap us in Jonesville – that we wouldn't get away in time to meet our friends. But, the wind died down just in time to leave Jonesville, make a quick stop in French Harbour for water, diesel fuel, and supplies and continue down to West End to meet up with Donna and Kathy.

What a thrill it is to share our lifestyle on this beautiful Caribbean Island with such good friends. Seeing it through Donna and Kathy's eyes gave us a new appreciation of the beauty of this place we are lucky enough to call home - for now! After a full day of sun and fun, swimming, snorkeling, and relaxing on the beach, John and I headed back to the boat for a rest before meeting the girls at Foster's in West End to enjoy a little nightlife.

Donna and Kathy had an introduction to the concept of island time when the 10:00 pm shuttle into town arrived at 11:00 pm. John and I have become accustomed to these delays and found a spot to wait and watch for the shuttle. We boogied to a variety of reggae and Latin music till 1:00 am, when the shuttle headed back to Henry Morgan's.

February 21

We spent Sunday morning strolling along the sandy beachfront road in West End, browsing in the touristy shops along the way, stopping for a cold drink and a swim for some relief from the heat. Thankfully the weather has cooperated and we have enjoyed sunny days with the cool, refreshing trade winds.

Back at the boat we enjoyed another swim and the captain put some lobster tails on the barbeque and threw together a delicious meal of Lobster Alfredo before the ladies headed back to their resort to freshen up and enjoy the evening entertainment.

Monday found us on our way into Coxen Hole, the capital of the island, for some souvenir shopping. We took the local bus for 20 *lempiras*, approximately $1.00 each and enjoyed the drive through the lush countryside. The gumbo limbo trees are in bloom and the hills are dotted with the mauve, lilac-like flowers, adding an extra special charm to the island for our guests.

Once again we hung out back at the boat, swam and relaxed on the aft deck with our million dollar view. John made us lobster quesadillas and I drove the girls back to their resort in West Bay, a short dinghy ride from the boat.

On Tuesday we met back down at West Bay to enjoy more snorkeling. Each spot we tried was better than the last. I took a plastic bottle filled with cracker crumbs to feed the fish and was swarmed by hundreds of them, only managing to snap a few pictures before chickening out and swimming away. We spotted a large parrotfish and I followed, trying to get close enough for pictures.

255

February 22

We've only seen bits and pieces of the island – most of it from the water. Several of our friends had suggested we take an island tour. With Donna and Kathy here, we decided it was the perfect time to explore the island.

While souvenir shopping in Coxen Hole, we met Raoul, a well-spoken, polite young man, who was trying to sell us trinkets on the street. I asked him if he sold island tours, which of course, he did.

We negotiated the terms. The girls didn't want to be packed into a hot, cramped taxi. We would be hopping in and out constantly. We needed room to pack a cooler, and air-conditioning would be a bonus.

"No problem," Raoul assured us. "I have just the van," he promised. We took his number and told him we'd call to confirm after we talked to John.

"Are you sure he has a van?" asked John, slightly dubious of our arrangements. "You know how they'll say anything you want to hear to get your business."

"Don't worry," I assured him. He promised us a van, with air-conditioning."

Sure enough, Raoul showed up at precisely 9:00 am Wednesday morning. We didn't recognize him at first, because he was driving a small, white car, like most of the vehicles on the island.

"Where is the van?" we asked. Raoul launched into what sounded like a long story, but the captain cut him off immediately.

"We've been on the island for a while," he said, "and we have seen it all, heard it all. If you don't have a van, just tell us and we will find someone who does."

Raoul made a few quick phone calls. He had found a van. It was not his but he would gladly take us into Coxen Hole and set us up with the driver of the van.

He was late for work, he told us, and drove like it. I tried to avoid John's eyes, knowing what he was thinking, as we sat through Honduran traffic jams with our guests in the hot, cramped taxi.

Once we arrived in Coxen Hole, sure enough there was a van waiting for us with a much more relaxed driver - a soft-spoken young man named Aquino. We loaded the cooler into the van and off we went.

Our first stop was our old stomping grounds of French Harbour. We toured the town and then stopped at the Roatan Yacht Club. I wanted to show the girls the magnificent view from the club, a place where I have spent much time since arriving on the island.

From there we headed east towards the quieter, less busy end of the island. We explored areas that John and I had not seen yet and enjoyed breathtaking views of the north shore of the island. We stopped in the little Garifuna town of Punta Gorda to stretch our legs and take pictures.

257

We decided to stop for lunch at Hole in the Wall, in Blue Rock, near Jonesville, another of our favorite spots. Donna and I shared a delicious seafood platter. Kathy had lobster cocktail and fries. John and Aquino savored cheeseburgers in paradise.

Of course, Hole in the Wall wouldn't be the same without a frosty rum punch and we enjoyed a couple before setting of with Clyde for a mangrove tour. Aquino, who has lived on the island for 21 years, had never been on a mangrove tour. The best part of the boat ride for me was hearing him squeal with delight as we rode the swell out on the open ocean on our way back to Jonesville.

It was a wonderful tour and we were exhausted when we returned to West End at the end of the day. We had showed our guests the "other Roatan", the less touristy east end of the island, as beautiful as West End, but in a different way.

February 23

Where does the time go? Thursday is here and it's my last day with Donna and Kathy. We packed a lot of fun and sun into the week and tried to show the girls as much of the island as possible while still finding time to relax.

The butterfly farm was a short walk from town. John insisted that he would prefer a little alone time on the boat and sent us off. He knows how much I miss my family and girlfriends and understands what this visit means to me.

There were as many tropical birds to see as there were butterflies and the tour was very informative. I didn't make notes so I cannot properly identify all the birds we saw but I did take lots of pictures.

Our friends Jim and Jeanie arrived in *Oasis I* shortly after we returned from the butterfly farm and I was anxious for them to meet Donna and Kathy. Fellow cruisers appreciate how special it is to have family and friends visit.

March 9

The plan when we left West End was to spend a couple of days in French Harbour. We would stock up on groceries and fuel before heading on to Jonesville to catch up on some internet.

It's been ten days now and we're still in French Harbour. We finally broke down and took a slip at the dock at Fantasy Island. We'd been on the hook for a solid two months at that point and were growing tired of listening to the generator, which needed to be run longer each day in order to charge the batteries.

In the old days, when we traveled a lot, the engine would charge our batteries. But here, on Roatan, with such short distances between destinations, we never run the engine long enough to fully charge our batteries. Therefore, shore power is necessary once in a while.

The timing was perfect, as a nasty front was forecast to come through, which it did, and nasty it was. We woke to the sound of the howling wind on our first night on the dock. John jumped out to add more bumpers to the boat.

"Where is the big flashlight? It looks like the Longs are behind us and I mean RIGHT behind us," he called out. Our friends Jim and Jeanie on *Oasis I* dragged anchor a few nights ago and endured the horrendous task of re-anchoring in the stormy darkness of night.

It was déjà vu, as we watched Jim struggle with his anchor. John shone the bright flashlight on them, trying to help.

"Oops! I just lit up Jim's bare ass!" he said

Poor Jim, I thought. Just what he needs when he has to run naked onto the bow to save his boat - some idiot shining a light on his bare ass.

I watched our friends re-anchor with a sick feeling in my stomach. It's easy to get hurt out there and I feared for them. They got the anchor re-set eventually and I slunk back to bed feeling guilty but safe at the dock.

I turned the radio on in case they called for help and sure enough, at 6:30 am, we got the call. They had been awake all night on anchor watch and wanted us to help them bring the boat into the dock. So, we caught their lines and helped them tie up. The water wasn't quite deep enough at the dock for their boat, and they sat on their keel much of the time, but at least they were safe.

That was the first night of the storm. Last night was quiet and we all slept well, until 5:30 this morning. The sound of wind clocking around 180 degrees is something you never forget and we both flew out of bed when we heard it.

Pearl, a boat anchored not far from us, was dragging and heading straight towards us. I heard Jeanie call them on the radio and they told her they were trying to re-set their anchor.

The force of the wind was so strong that all three of our bumpers popped out from between the dock and the boat, leaving *Diamond Lil* banging against a piling. I jumped out to help John stuff the bumpers back in, but we weren't strong enough, so I ran down the dock to get help.

Boaters always help each other and before long we had a crowd pushing *Diamond Lil* away from the dock to allow us to add several more bumpers. Jim and the fellow from behind us reached down and hauled our dinghy up onto the dock, as it was crashing around in the waves.

The radio waves were alive with boaters who were dragging and other boaters offering assistance. Both boats behind us had just picked up company from the airport yesterday and I thought to myself that they must surely think we are all nuts, living this life. Most of the time it is paradise but sometimes you have to pay the price.

A few hours can make all the difference and now I sit looking out at paradise once again. It's still windy, though. We couldn't leave the dock yet if we tried. We

have resigned ourselves to paying for our slip at
Fantasy Island for another night.

When the dust settled from the storm, there was a
sailboat washed up on the reef. The couple onboard did
not fare as well in the storm, when they missed the
somewhat tricky entrance to the anchorage.

They were fined for damaging the reef. Apparently they
had no boat documentation, nor could they afford to pay
the fine. Rumor has it they were offered $2,000.00 for
the boat, took it, and ran.

We finally made it over to visit the Arch family's Iguana
Farm. It is one of the most popular tourist attractions
on the island and is only a few hundred feet from where
we were anchored. The Arch family of French Key has
been working for years to save the endangered iguanas
on the island. Iguana stew is one of the favorite local
dishes. The place wasn't really a farm, just a fenced
property, crawling with about 3,000 of the beasts.

There, we ran into two couples that we met in the
Bahamas - one last winter in Georgetown and one the
winter before in Marsh Harbour. Power boats are in the
minority here, so when they had spotted *Diamond Lil*,
they remembered her.

We attended a pot luck happy-hour on shore here at
Fantasy Island a couple of nights ago. Friends from the
Rio have just arrived and the weather has everyone held
captive, but we know how to look at the bright side.

March 11

Our plan, when we left the dock at Fantasy Island yesterday, was to head to Jonesville for a few days of catching up on the internet, then east to the island of Guanaja. At the last minute, we decided to head west instead, back to West End. We find ourselves here once again and I can't complain.

A mooring ball came open this morning and we zipped over and tied up to it. It is much safer than our anchor, if the weather turns bad.

The captain finally broke down and removed our old microwave which had stopped working and went off in search of a new one. We have been humming and hawing about it for a month. Every time we decided to buy a new one, the old one would work for a few more days.

John spent hours searching. We wanted a black microwave so it would match the other appliances. We needed a certain size, to fit the opening in the wall. Finally, he found the ONLY black microwave that was the right size for our galley on the island, in Coxen Hole. He returned to the boat and told me about it. I called to make sure it was still there before we headed all the way back to town.

Despite the assurance that it was still there, by the time we rode the mini-van bus, from West End to Coxen Hole, and walked to the store, the microwave oven was gone.

"Sorry. I sold it half an hour ago," the clerk apologized.

We had to settle for a silver model that was smaller than the old one. Yes, the store took our Visa credit card. But, the power was out, so the Visa machine wouldn't work.

So, John stood in line at the bank for ages to withdraw cash, during which time the power went off and on about ten times.

March 12

This morning John installed the new microwave. It is much smaller and doesn't have a back mounting system like the old one and he had to make some modifications. In town he found a guy he knows who sold him a small piece of wood from his construction site. Projects require much ingenuity here – there is no Home Depot or anything else even remotely similar. As usual, my Captain Fix-It came through with flying colors.

March 19

Santa Semana, or Easter week, is the busiest time of year in Roatan. Hondurans from the mainland and tourists from Central and South America flock to the beaches to celebrate the Easter weekend in a ritual somewhat like our May 24th weekend.

There are many religious celebrations held, but in West End the atmosphere is much more like Wasaga Beach, Ontario. Families, couples, and crowds of young people descend upon the town. Store and business owners are busy adding fresh coats of paint to their buildings and fences. Several new establishments literally opened up just in time for the big week. Places that we have walked past for months, without seeing a soul, were packed solid with patrons. Most of our favorite eating spots had no tables to spare.

It made for an interesting week of people watching. We found ourselves out at Foster's dancing until 3:30 a.m., closer to when we usually wake up than go to bed. I have created a monster. I could barely drag the captain out on to the dance floor in the past. I'm not sure if it's the combination of hot blooded Latin, soca and reggae music has made a new man out of him or the combination of hot blooded, scantily clad women on the dance floor.

We explored along the north coast by dinghy one day, up past Anthony's Key and Sandy Bay. Once we passed this busy tourist area and headed further east there were huge undeveloped areas of country and miles of empty shoreline. We rescued three young boys who had floated away from their family in a little dinghy and towed them back.

All the boaters were caught off guard when a much stronger front than anticipated arrived on Easter weekend. We had snagged the best mooring ball in the harbor and rode the storm out with no problems. However, two other mooring balls were pulled out of the ground in the storm and the boaters had to quickly drop their anchors to avoid being washed up on the reef.

Jamie, in front of his boat *DIVERS AT PLAY*, in French Harbour

John, Jim and Jeanie (left) and Sharon and Joe (right) at Gio's

Beautiful sunset over the town of French Harbour, Roatan

Crystal clear water in the anchorage at French Harbour Cay

A pig's head for sale on the street in French Harbour

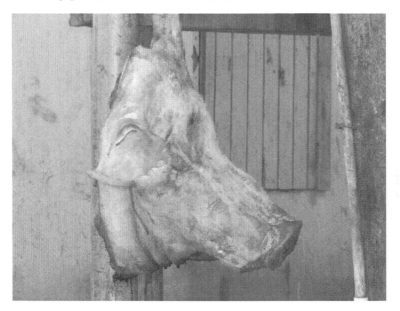

Hole In the Wall Bar and Restaurant in Blue Rock, Roatan

Hole In the Wall in Blue Rock, Roatan

Enjoying the Sunday afternoon barbeque buffet at The Hole

Abagado likes the food too

There is always a basket full of free cigars at Hole In the Wall

The Float N Sip Bar, in Jonesville Bight, Roatan

Diamond Lil, anchored in front of Woodside Marina, Jonesville

Merry Christmas from Roatan – making calls to family at home

Stilt houses in Oak Ridge, Roatan

273

Climbing back down the hill on the road behind Mr. Larry's house

Enjoying our walk and the view from the top of the hill

Taking a shower, compliments of Mother Nature, in Jonesville

Jim and Jeanie, in the pool at Fantasy Island, French Harbour Cay

The view of the west end of the island from *Diamond Lil*

At Denny's Restaurant in West End – finding an internet signal

John, on the dock at Ronnie's Beach Bar, West End, Roatan

West End sunset

277

Diamond Lil, beside another Bayliner at French Harbour Yacht Club

John, driving the dinghy in West End

278

There is a pot of gold in Roatan

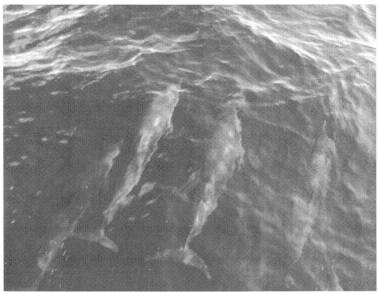

Wherever we go, the dolphins follow us

Anchored in front of the Float N Sip Bar, Jonesville, Roatan

Mr. Bob (front) with his sidekicks – Harry (right) and Dwayne (left)

John, with Donna (middle) and Kathy (front) in West End

Dancing with Donna and Kathy at Fosters in West End

Chapter 12

Guanaja, Honduras Bay Islands

March 24, 2007

We looked up at each other over coffee this morning, read each other's minds, and said "Let's go to Guanaja."

About an hour later we were on our way to visit the third of the Honduras Bay Islands. Even when we are leaving somewhere as fabulous as West End, it is still a thrill to get underway. We've been in the Bay Islands for about 3 ½ months now, and I'm excited to be heading into new waters and on our way to explore a new island.

We planned to take advantage of a small weather window to travel to Guanaja. The long trip would charge our batteries and we would arrive just as the winds were forecast to pick up.

John ran into West End in the dinghy for some ice so we could fish along the way. I readied the boat to leave. We were on our way by 8:30 am, enjoying a leisurely five-hour cruise to the most easterly of the three islands.

We caught our one and only fish in about 100 feet of water as we entered the shallower area surrounding Guanaja. It felt a lot bigger than it was and took about 15 minutes to reel in. It turned out to be half a fish. Some larger fish had eaten the tail end of it so it didn't glide through the water, but came in like a dead weight.

Plan A had been to head for Graham's Place on Josh's

Cay, an appealing place we had heard about that
provides free water and ice to boaters, has laundry
facilities, and internet. Those are a lot of features to find
in the same place in the islands.

Plan B went into place when the wind picked up from
the northeast, which we knew would make the
anchorage at Josh's Cay uncomfortable. El Bight, about
five miles closer, provides great protection from wind
from all directions. Here we are, tucked in safe and
sound along with four or five sailboats.

March 26

Physically, the island of Guanaja is what I imagined a
tropical paradise would be, and yet it is so much more.
Almost everyone we meet asks how we like it here. Then
they tell their story of coming to the island, and in many
cases, of staying here.

"It's a hard place to leave," is what we hear most often.
We believe it. The island is unique in that it has few, if
any real roads or automobiles.

The island of Guanaja is approximately 25 kilometres
long by 4 kilometres wide. However, about 80% of the
population lives on what appears to be one small island.
It began as two small cays that were joined together
over time to form Bonacca.

Bonacca is also known as Guanaja Town but most of the
locals simply call it "the cay." It is home to about 8,000
people, living in an area of roughly ten acres. Sometimes
it is referred to as the Venice of the Caribbean.
Apparently there are more people per square mile living
here than in Hong Kong.

In places, the original narrow canals run between the buildings, but most have been filled in with cement and made into narrow walkways.

At first, Bonacca appears to be a maze. Eventually, we found our way around. In the beginning we would follow the twisty little paths between buildings and discover a series of dead ends. Few stores are marked with signs, nor are any of the little streets.

Bonacca is a stilt town, similar to many other settlements in the islands, but the stilts here are anchored on a submerged shoal. Densely clustered wooden buildings, painted in bright tropical colors, give the island a shimmery, mirage-like appearance from a distance.

Everyone here knows each other, so we immediately stood out as visitors. The townsfolk were more than friendly, going out of their way to stop and chat with us. They were curious about where we were from, where we were staying, and how we liked it here.

English was the original language on Guanaja, as it was in all the Bay Islands. However, more and more Spanish speaking people have moved over from the mainland. We heard a pretty equal mix of the two languages spoken on the cay.

The famous landmark of Dunbar's Rock lies between El Bight, where we are anchored, and Bonacca. To our north, and stretching from east to west, is the main island of Guanaja, the tallest of all the Honduras Bay Islands. It is also the least visited island. There are no crowds and no hotel-lined beaches. In fact, on our first walk around Bonacca, we saw virtually no other gringos.

Before long we will get used to it again, but after leaving West End, where we blended in with all the other tourists, it does seem odd.

Guanaja was named by Christopher Columbus when he first set foot on the island in 1502. It means land of pines. Covered in Caribbean Pine, it was at that time the most heavily wooded of the three islands.

Hurricane Mitch devastated the island in 1989 and much of the forest was lost. The worst of the damage was on the north coast, which we have not seen yet. But even on this south coast, it is mind boggling to see huge swatches of empty mountainside with just a few bare trunks standing, surrounded by thick, dense, untouched forest.

March 26

The wind finally died down and we made a run for Josh's Cay. This was our intended destination before windy weather and rough seas sent us scurrying for the protection of El Bight.

Graham is a flavorful character from the Cayman Islands who is living his dream on his own private island. We have heard it described as a Garden of Eden. Deer, rabbits, and peacocks wander free. Four large penned-in areas of seawater contain sea turtles, an enormous jewfish, a nurse shark, several stingrays, and a wide variety of fish. Feeding time makes for great entertainment.

March 27

Outside the boat, we are anchored in yet another turquoise paradise. Inside the boat, the air is as blue as the water she lies in. The captain and I tried several times to start the generator, but to no avail. We have had trouble starting it for about a week, but today it was just plain dead. John checked the water pump, discovered a stream of water gushing from it, and was not happy.

"That's it. We'll have to head back to Guanaja and find somewhere on shore to take it apart. I can't work on it here."

"The internet isn't working anyway," I replied. We can come back here another time."

March 30

"Do you hear that?" I asked John

"The music, you mean?" he asked me.

"Yes. I've heard that before at this time of night. It's a Beatles song. They're all English songs - old ones. Where do you suppose it's coming from?"

"I've seen boats coming in and out of the bay over there. There must be a bar or restaurant over there on shore. Let's follow the music and find out where it's coming from," said hubby.

Following the sound of the music, we came to a large, open-fronted building, with a wide set of grey, wooden steps in the middle of it. Above the steps hung a sign that read "Manati Bar and Restaurant." We climbed the steps and were swept into the crowd.

Timing is everything. We had stumbled into the middle of a birthday party for Hansito, owner of the Manati. Like many of the folks on the island of Guanaja, Hansito is originally from Germany.

"Velcome. Velcome. Sit. Sit," said Florian, a cheerful, round-cheeked fellow, quite obviously also from Germany.

"Ve are having a birthday. Eat, eat. Today, for the fiesta, there is no charge. You must stay. Velcome," said Florian.

How could we resist? We found a small table with a view of *Diamond Lil* bobbing peacefully in the anchorage of El Bight. A tiny woman hustled over to our table and introduced herself as Annette. She had her long brown hair tied back and wore a floor-length cotton sun-dress. Her feet were bare.

She and her husband ran the place, she told us, as she called him over to the table and introduced us. Klaus was tall and thin, with sharp features and blonde hair. She and her husband, Klaus, were from Germany, she told us. Surprise -surprise. I felt like we had rowed to shore and landed in Germany.

We feasted on delicious grilled pork roast, homemade German potato salad, and fresh, homemade bread. An amazing assortment of musicians entertained us. Most of them were from Germany, one guy was from England, and several were locals. The friendliness of this crowd was overwhelming. Nearly everyone introduced themselves to us and several invited us to their homes, here on the island.

287

April 5

"You've heard that the definition of cruising is fixing your boat in exotic locations," came the familiar remark from Brian, who was perched on a bar stool to our right.

We met Brian the first night we stumbled into the place, but I haven't heard him say much. He is a quiet guy. He stands medium height and has sandy brown hair, which is starting to grey. He's a good looking guy, but it seems like he hasn't seen a hairbrush in a while.

Brian is the friend that Mr. Larry was telling us about back in Roatan – the one whose old sailboat had been made into the base for the Float N Sip, the local whorehouse.

He too is Canadian, far from his home of Alberta, now living on his sailboat *Ketch 22*, in El Bight. He has the look of a confirmed bachelor.

"Lucky guy," said John.

"Why? Because his boat is now a whorehouse or because he's a bachelor?" I asked.

"Because he has no nagging wife to tell him what to wear or bitch at him to brush his hair," he said.

We had just bellied up to the bar at our recently discovered gringo hangout and John was telling the tale of our broken Westerbeke generator.

The captain struck up a conversation with a man named Hans Pico, also from Germany, who has been living on the island for 30 years. He was not much taller than me, with long, white-blonde hair that he wore pulled back in

a ponytail. The ponytail stuck out through the hole in
the back of his tattered ball cap. His moustache and
eyebrows were the same white-blonde color as his hair.
It was his voice, with the thick German accent, that
really stood out, though.

Hans offered to phone two diesel mechanics that he
knew. Finding one would be faster for him, he assured
us. He, as a local, would get a better price than we
would, as a couple of touristy-looking gringos.

He warned us that there was a good chance both
mechanics would be booked solid with work, however.
Lobster season had just ended and the fleet of fishing
boats had returned for maintenance and repairs.

April 6

Hans called bright and early. As he had feared, neither
diesel mechanic had the time to help us. So, hubby
decided to repair the water pump himself. Once again
Hans came to our rescue. He offered the services of a
contact of his in La Ceiba, a large city on the Honduran
mainland, to hunt down the parts we needed for our
Jabsco water pump and ship them to Guanaja by air.

I am squeezed into a tiny cubicle at an internet café on
the island of Bonacca. We love Guanaja more and more
each day. We have met many expats from Canada, the
U.S., and Germany. Most are from Germany. We hear
more German these days than Spanish and the
helpfulness of these people is unbelievable.

My trip to the internet café on the cay has proved
worthwhile today, for I have a message from my
daughter, Suzanne. She and her boyfriend, Russ, are
flying to Roatan on May 1st for a short visit and I am
thrilled.

They visited us on the boat in the Bahamas last winter, and we had a great time. The captain is happy because when I am happy I clean. Have I been cleaning! Luckily there is no shortage of things to clean on a boat.

Luckily also, there is no shortage of fresh, pure water on this island and best of all it's FREE! Each day John fills up our jugs from a tap on shore and brings it back to the boat. I fill the bathtub and wash our clothes and hang them to dry. The refreshing trade wind blows constantly and dries the laundry quickly.

April 8

Today, Hans dropped by on his way back from the cay with our water pump parts. Before he finished the cold beer that we offered him, John had the pump put back together and installed in the boat.

I stood up in the cabin and held the glow switch for 30 seconds and turned her over. No go. I glowed and cranked and glowed and cranked. John and Hans were both down in the hatch by this time. They tried spraying some Quick Start on the intake. More glowing, more cranking - the sounds were awful coming from down in the hatch.

I stayed out of the way and did what I usually do - took pictures and video footage. Later I will edit out the parts where the captain barks, "Enough," or "Now you're really getting ridiculous," or whatever. I slink away quietly and then when he's not looking, I casually go back to my filming. He'll thank me some day.

With the two guys climbing in and out of the hatch, digging further and further into the oily generator, I couldn't stay totally out of the way. I followed them with hot, soapy rags to take the marks off poor *Diamond Lil.*

She isn't just a boat of course, she's our home and oil
marks do not come out of some of her surfaces easily.

I spread towels and old sheets over our light beige
carpet. I laid sheets over our beige seats that they would
stop to sit in while discussing their theories. I heard
them talking about pulling it all apart and had visions
of oily parts scattered all over my precious boat.

April 9

John suspects trouble with the head gasket, the heat
exchanger, or both. Hans has offered the use of his
beautiful ocean-view piece of land, with a dock for our
dinghy, tables to work on, and electricity. Electricity is
essential for the power tools that hubby needs for the
job. He has decided to dismantle the generator and
transport it, in pieces, to shore by dinghy. There, he will
have peace and quiet and I won't be reaching between
his legs, cleaning while he works.

What a relief to me. He can putter away happily on
shore. He can take his oily, greasy rags and all the open
containers of oil, which I visualize tipping over in a big
wake. He can take his boxes and boxes of tools over to
his little workshop in paradise.

Again, Hans called his contact in La Ceiba and asked
him to investigate the availability of Westerbeke parts
on the mainland. In case we couldn't find the parts here
in Honduras, he also brought us a phone number for
Mavex Corp in Miami, a business he has ordered boat
parts successfully from, in the past.

The damage to our generator was caused by the raw
water pump, which had leaked saltwater into the oil.
John determined this by tasting the oil, which makes

me glad I'm not a guy. The compression seemed poor, which led him to believe that the head gasket was worn, but there was no way to test it accurately out here in this remote cruising destination.

The generator would have to come apart. Only then would he know what was wrong with it. When we removed the cylinder head, it was gummed up and full of carbon. It appeared that antifreeze had been seeping through from the exhaust manifold. Once the head was disassembled, we discovered that the valve stems and seats were badly pitted.

John also suspected that the heat exchanger was leaking. He removed the end piece, fashioned a simple pressure tester from a bicycle inner tube, and filled it full of soapy water. Luckily, there were no leaks so all we need are two new end gaskets and a new zinc pencil. We carry several spare pencils.

John also noticed that the aluminum at one end of the exhaust manifold had been corroded by the saltwater. For this job his J&B Weld came to the rescue.

"I'll need a few coats," he explained. "Each coat will take a day to dry, so we'll have to be patient."

"Be patient! You're kidding me. At this rate, we'll never get to back Roatan to meet Suzanne and Russ."

He ground the powder out and ended up with a larger hole, which he then filled in with the first coat of JB Weld.

"I don't know," said Hans, shaking his head. "I think you should just order a new exhaust manifold."

Hans' cell phone chirped to life, but the news is not
good. The Westerbeke parts we need are not available
on the mainland. We will have to order them from the
U.S.

April 10

John is at his post, sitting on the settee, in front of our
captain's table. He has a cup of steaming coffee in hand
and his list of parts in front of him, as he places a call to
the Mavex Corp in Miami. We need...

One head gasket
Two end gaskets for the exhaust manifold
Two end gaskets for the heat exchanger
Three intake valves
Three exhaust valves
Six valve seals
Two lift pump elements
Two secondary fuel filters
One impeller kit for the water pump (as a spare since
we had just installed our spare)

"I'm sorry sir, but you don't have a very good line.
You'll have to call back when you can get a better
connection," said the clerk on the Miami end of the
phone.

"DON'T HANG UP!" pleaded John. "This IS a good line.
I'm calling from Honduras and I have been trying to get
through for about 40 minutes."

The phone system in Honduras is not what we are used
to in Canada or the U.S. Sometimes you get through,
often you don't. The captain doesn't normally make
phone calls – he jokes that it's why he married me. I
make almost all the phone calls. But these are boat

parts we are ordering – serious business – and thankfully for me, he is taking care of it.

He finally convinced the party at the other end of the line that this scratchy connection was the best he was going to get. He recited off the make and model of our generator, along with the serial number.

"I'm sorry sir," replied the clerk, as he fed the information into his computer, "But there is no such model in existence."

"Well, I'm looking at it," said John, "and I have the owner's manual and parts list from your company, with a picture of our generator on it so it certainly DOES exist."

It is a 1985 model so I figured it probably wasn't in the kid's computer.

"The only way I can search for the parts, sir, is if you email me a picture of the serial number. I cannot hear you clearly enough to take the information over the phone."

"You'll never be able to make it out in the pictures," grumbled John, "But I'll see what we can do."

I snapped several close-up photos of the serial number. I quickly uploaded them on to my laptop to demonstrate to my agitated husband that we could see them clearly. The idiot who was not able to take the numbers over the phone would be able to make them out.

The dinghy ride to Bonacca to use the internet café is extremely rough. After making the trip several times, we have decided that it is prudent to leave our laptop safely back at the boat. So, I loaded the pictures onto a memory stick. John scanned the picture of our generator from the manual, along with the schematic drawings of all the components we needed parts for.

He indicated on each printout which part number we needed. We made it so clear that surely the parts company couldn't possibly mess up the order.

April 11

We called Miami this morning to confirm that our email had been received. It had and apparently all the parts are available. We must dinghy back into town, however, to confirm the order by email and provide our Visa number. It wasn't possible to take it by phone, the people at Mavex insisted.

Off we went again, braving the enormous waves and swell rolling through the harbor. The email reply listing the parts we needed showed only one of each fuel filter required, so we wrote once again, asking for two, not one of each filter. We followed up the email with a phone call, and we were assured that all was in order. The parts would be shipped by FedEx from Miami to San Pedro Sula, a large city on the Honduran mainland, and from there to La Ceiba.

From La Ceiba the package would fly via Sosa Airlines to Guanaja, since FedEx service does not extend to the island. The total cost for these parts is about $560.00 U.S. We have no idea what the cost of shipping them all over the place will be, nor how long it will take.

It's Friday and finally our order has been placed. We are having fantasies of receiving our parts by the middle of the next week. John explained how back in the 'real world' where he worked as an auto mechanic, the parts would often be delivered on either the same or at the very least, the next day.

Living on the boat has been a little more challenging than usual without our generator. The only way to charge the batteries is to run our engines, which really isn't good for them. We have been using as little battery power as possible, which has cut down on our computer usage. Luckily we have a little two-burner propane camp stove to cook on and make coffee in the morning.

We can make hot water by running the port side engine. But for dishes, laundry, and cleaning it is more economical to boil it on our little stove.

April 14

Each morning, we drive the dinghy over to shore to work on the generator. First, we douse ourselves with a heavy coating of OFF bug spray. I wander around taking pictures and playing with Hans' dog, staying close by for when my hands are needed. John sands and coats and sands and coats his exhaust manifold and waits and waits for each coat to dry so he can sand some more.

Every couple of days, we brave the trip into town in our inflatable dinghy to check our FedEx tracking number online. One day, when the weather was too rough for us to make it to the Cay, we called Suzanne, at home in Canada and had her track the shipment for us. I led her through the Spanish FedEx website for tracking in Honduras and she was able to pull up the information for us. The package had made it as far as San Pedro Sula and was due to ship to La Ceiba in the morning. YES!

Tourists are few and far between in Guanaja. I was told once that at any given time there are about ten tourists on this island, with the numbers swelling to about 20 during the busy Easter week! Compare that with probably tens of thousands of tourists on Roatan, at least in the winter.

Twelve year-old Tony has become our regular boat boy when we are in Bonacca. We have been in Bonacca a lot this last week. He helps us carry the groceries, keeps an eye on our dinghy for us while we shop, and helps us find what we are looking for in town.

In return, we give him a few *lempiras*. His dad passed away recently, leaving him and his Mom. He is a sweet, polite boy, fluent in both English and Spanish.

April 15

I called the FedEx office in La Ceiba this morning and spoke to the person most fluent in English. This turned out to be better than my Spanish, but not by much.

The shipment could not be forwarded to the island, she explained, until the payment was received in La Ceiba. I would have to either go to La Ceiba or have someone there make the payment for me.

Since we don't know a soul in La Ceiba and are not about to spend considerable time and money to travel there, I carefully took as much information from her as I could.

Then we headed back into Bonacca. We asked at the *Banca Atlantida*, the only bank in Bonacca, if there was a way to make a deposit to the FedEx account.

"We cannot deposit to that account," explained the bank teller. "It's a different bank. There is no way."

The people in Guanaja will go to great lengths to be of assistance to us and Donna in the Sosa Airlines office in Bonacca went out of her way to help.

We explained our dilemma and Donna picked up the phone and called the FedEx woman in La Ceiba. She explained, in Spanish, what we were trying to do. After a long conversation, of which I understood about one-third, Donna explained that although this was "strictly prohibito," she was going to do us a favour and make an exception.

We followed her from the office to the bank, about 11 steps down the narrow walkway and around a corner. She waited patiently in the line with me, on her own time, until a teller was free. The banks are very slow here and it is not uncommon to line up for one or two hours, or even longer.

Thankfully, the wait was not long today, and Donna explained that she was going to deposit our money in a friend's account in La Ceiba. The friend was going to withdraw the money for us, walk to the FedEx office and make the payment.

April 16

When we called FedEx in La Ceiba this morning, we were assured that the payment had been made and the shipment cleared.

"We cannot take it to the airport," the clerk explained to me, "Because the roads are taken."

"What do you mean the roads are taken?" I asked.

She explained that there was a general strike on the mainland and the roads were taken, which I took to mean closed or blocked. Strikes are illegal in Honduras, but the workers had joined together anyway and our package was going nowhere fast! And here we had hoped that the package would be on the weekly supply ship tomorrow.

April 17

Finally, it's Thursday - ship day - and alas, our parts are hung up on the mainland. We had no plans for the day, and we decided to go into town for lunch even though the parts have not arrived. While I was at the internet café, the captain just happened to pop into the Sosa Airlines office to see what Donna knew about the strike. She told him, much to his relief that our package was on the way and would be here in a few hours.

Thursday in Bonacca is like a three ring circus. That is the day that the weekly supply boat from the mainland comes in and people show up from all over to pick up shipments of all shapes and sizes.

John sat with our groceries at the Sosa office and waited while I traipsed down to the dock to take pictures. The dock was a flurry of activity as families loaded appliances and sacks of flour and rice onto their *launches*, or *pangas* as they are sometimes called here in the Bay Islands.

Huge stacks of merchandise were piled on the dock for the larger stores, with smaller stacks for the smaller *tiendas*. There, lying by itself on the dock, surrounded by mayhem, was a small, white FedEx box.

Sure enough, the fellow from Sosa showed up, claimed the package, processed some paperwork, and motioned me to follow him back to the office. We buzzed back to *Diamond Lil* and the captain tore into the package. It took the two of us about five minutes to open the package - it was that well wrapped.

Despite the captain's diligence in sending explicit diagrams, we had been shipped two incorrect gaskets and were missing three of four fuel filters. We had paid for the gaskets and one of the filters, so of $533.20 on our invoice, $50.80 was for items we hadn't received.

After waiting a week for the parts, John decided to make do with what we had and try to have the charges for the items not received refunded to our Visa card. The head gasket and the valves which were the crucial parts were correct. He could make gaskets for the exhaust manifold himself and would just have to do without one new fuel filter. The other missing two filters were going to be spares, and we could buy them later.

April 18

Back to shore we went, with all the tools and parts and John went to work. He worked from 8:00 am till 6:00 pm, reassembling the cylinder head and then reinstalling it into the boat.

April 19

After changing the oil this morning, it was the moment of truth. Would she run? Once again I glowed while he cranked. This time the beast started and she never sounded as sweet.

For the first time in three weeks we can use our stove, our toaster, our vacuum, our laptops, and our blender – all the things we take for granted when the beast is

working. We can charge our batteries without running
our diesel engine and life can return to normal.

April 23

In just over a week, Russ and Suzanne will arrive. As
much as we hate to leave Guanaja, we can't wait for
them to get here. We docked outside Zapata's General
store, on Bonacca, to stock up on a few items. I enjoyed
one last breakfast at my favorite little restaurant. I
snapped a photo of my plate of scrambled eggs, refried
beans, tortillas, fried hot dogs, a hunk of dry white
cheese, and a small container of strange looking butter.

An enjoyable, three-hour cruise had us pulling into
French Harbour just in time to be invited out to dinner
with a group of boaters that we knew from the Rio
Dulce. We gathered in the parking lot at Fantasy
Island, piling into SUVs and the back of a pickup truck.

"What a life," I said to John, as 18 of us gathered around
the candlelit table at Gio's, in French Harbour.

We left a bunch of great new friends in Guanaja, just
this morning. Here we are, just a few hours later,
surrounded by more friends. What an amazing life we
lead.

Apr 30

After a week in French Harbour, spent shopping and
cleaning and spending time with friends, we cruised the
short 17-miles to West End. We will pick Suzanne and

Russ up at the airport by taxi and bring them back to the anchorage here. We even found our favorite mooring ball free. What a stroke of luck!

May 1

After a month of waiting, they are finally here. I watched from the inside of the terminal as Suzanne descended the steps from the plane. John snapped a picture of me, in my new lime-green cotton shirt that I bought in Coxen Hole.

I watched them feed their luggage through the scanner. Russ held a huge box. They have arrived bearing gifts - items from Canada that we cannot buy down here.

We loaded up the taxi and set out along the beautiful drive to West End.

"I love the way the roads twist and turn all over the place, for no apparent reason," said Suzanne, and I laughed.

"They twist and turn and wind like this because of the mountains," I teased her and we all laughed.

The kids have brought a beautiful new stainless steel boat grill, my Mother's Day gift. I am touched. I told Suzanne, in a telephone conversation last week, how John had been hunting all over the island for a new barbeque, with no luck.

Our old grill had been the victim of a boating accident. I was cleaning it out on the swim platform one day, when a huge wake hit. I watched it plummet to the bottom of the sea.

"Oh, oh," I said.

"What?" asked John from inside the boat. I had no good answer for him so I didn't say anything.

"You didn't?" he said, as he walked out to see what had happened, noticing the sheepish look on my face.

All is well now. We have a beautiful new boat grill, which we initiated with a feast of lobster.

May 2

With our dinghy tied to our mooring ball, to show arriving boaters that it was already taken, we headed out in the big boat to do a little fishing.

"Are you sure you should drink that?" I asked Suzanne, as she snapped open the lid on a can of cold beer. I knew she tended to get a little seasick.

"It's calm out here today," she said. "I feel great."

And it was calm. It always is, just off West End, but as soon as you round the end of the island, the sea becomes choppy. I'd made the trip several times, and I was a little worried about her.

We lurched and rolled and I watched the color slowly drain from her face. Russ noticed too, and suggested that perhaps we should head in and try again on a calmer day.

We returned to the mooring ball, marked by our rubber dinghy.

"Why don't you load the rods and tackle into the dinghy?" suggested John.

"The reef is right there, and beyond it the water is deep. You can catch fish right there and Suzanne won't be seasick."

Russ busied himself tying lures and loading the dinghy. Off they went, with a cooler bag full of cold beer.

"Someone accidentally put some paper in the head," said John. "I'm going to have to take it apart to get it unplugged. It's going to be nasty and I didn't want to embarrass them. That's why I sent them off fishing."

Poor John, I thought. I stood well out of the way as he rushed through the cabin, with a green garbage bag wrapped around the dripping head. He returned with his plumber's snake – something we've had to use more than once, and got back to the grisly task.

Of course, Mr. Fix-It found the clog and removed it. I cleaned the head while he cleaned the floor where it had been. In no time, the head was restored to its sparkling condition. The tools were put away and we sat down, just as the kids returned.

"Mom," shouted Suzanne, standing in the dinghy as she neared the boat.

"Look what Russ caught. We're not sure what it is, but it's pretty big."

I snapped a couple of shots of Suzanne and Russ, standing on the swim platform with big smiles on their faces, in front of their fine kingfish.

"So, what did you guys do, while we were out fishing?" asked Suzanne, as we dined on a meal of jerk kingfish. I felt John kick my foot, under the table.

"Oh. Not much," I said.

There are few sights to match a West End sunset from our swim platform. Slowly, the giant orange ball dips below the blackening sea, until it is no more than a tiny crescent, and then it is gone!

Suzanne styled my hair and we changed into our evening wear. Well, the kids changed into their evening wear. We pulled on our best boat outfits and set off for Foster's.

"Wait until you hear the great music they play here," I told Suzanne. It's impossible not to dance to it.

"Mom · are you kidding me? Please tell me you don't think this music is new. They've been playing this in the clubs at home for years," my daughter told me.

May 4

Squeezing the four of us and Suzanne and Russ's luggage into the rubber dinghy, we headed for the dock at Ronnie's Beach Bar. The beach seemed unusually quiet as we arrived on shore.

"Good morning," said Ronnie. He was a short, Honduran man, who always wore a big smile.

"Good morning Ronnie," I said. "We arranged for a taxi yesterday, but I don't see it yet."

"That's because all the roads are closed," Ronnie told me, still smiling. "The running part of the triathlon event is today, so all the roads are closed."

"Oh no," I moaned. "We need to get my daughter and her boyfriend to the airport. Their flight leaves around noon."

"Ma'am," I heard from behind me. There was only one vehicle parked in Ronnie's beachside parking lot – a van, which sat idling.

"I know someone. I can make a phone call and get your guests to the airport," said the man.

Relief washed over me as he placed a call on his cell phone and motioned for us to hop into his comfortable, air-conditioned van.

His seemed to be the only vehicle on the road. We arrived at the airport in record time. The time had flown by much too quickly and we hated to see the kids go.

"It's ok Mom. Don't be sad," said Suzanne, as we kissed good-bye. "You're coming home in a couple of weeks. I'll see you then."

"Can we just stay until their plane takes off?" I asked John.

"NO. We can't just stay until their plane takes off. Come on, Mel. Say good-bye and get in the van before

the driver takes off and we end up walking back to West
End."

The half a fish we caught on our way to Guanaja

Diamond Lil, anchored in front of beautiful Graham's Place

The Manati Bar and Restaurant, El Bight, Guanaja

John, at the bar at the Manati

Dunbar Rock, Guanaja

The island of Guanaja

One of the narrow little alleyways on Bonacca

Hans Pico, who bent over backwards to help us with our generator

John, removing the heat exchanger from the generator

Tony, our Bonaccan boat boy

John, taking the generator and all his tools to shore

Hans generously offered his place for John to work on the generator

Spraying the cylinder head with oven cleaner – as good as degreaser

This is how the snacks come here – with bags you cut apart yourself

Thursday in Bonacca is ship day. Where is our FedEx package?

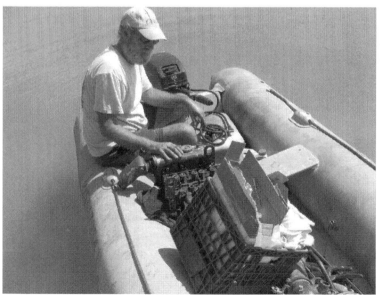

Transporting the repaired generator parts back to *Diamond Lil*

Yes, men DO read owner's manuals

Bonacca, as seen from a distance

Posing with my new stainless steel boat grill from Russ and Suzanne

Looking very happy to have the kids here with us in Roatan

Heading out to sea for a little fishing

Russ and Suzanne, returning from a ride in the dinghy in West End

John, Suzanne, and Russ in the dinghy in West End

John, Russ, and Suzanne on the beach in West Bay

Russ and Suzanne with their kingfish, in West End, Roatan

Enjoying a cold one at Sundowner's in West End, Roatan

Chapter 13

Back to the Rio

June 4, 2008

It's not easy leaving Paradise. The Bay Islands are my favorite of all the places we've traveled to on *Diamond Lil* over the past three years, so saying good-bye to return to the Rio Dulce for hurricane season is bittersweet. We know that these little gems of islands are waiting for us here next year, a mere 170 miles away. We'll miss the clear turquoise waters, white beaches, thick, lush vegetation and most of all, the friendliest people we have ever met.

French Harbour has been home for the past month or so. It's the prettiest anchorage of them all at night, I think. The town stretches up over the hills and as darkness falls the lights come on, dotting the hillsides in the distance. It reminds me of the Jamaican landscape at night and I never tire of it. This is where we spent our first night in Roatan. Much has happened since then.

We filled our water tank at Fantasy Island, said goodbye to some friends, and motored to the shrimp boat dock in old French Harbour. We asked these kind people, who have been allowing the cruisers to use their docks for our dinghies, if we could please dock *Diamond Lil* there for about an hour, in order to haul our jerry cans up to the gas station for diesel fuel. The prices have been soaring here and the island has suffered a diesel shortage. The place where we bought fuel the last time no longer has any for sale. Fantasy Island is not selling fuel any longer either, as they need to keep every bit they can get for their own use.

We waved good-bye to the children on shore and headed out to sea. Plan A was to travel as far as Utila and spend the first night there. Our outboard motor is broken AGAIN, so we have decided not to bother trying to get to shore along the way back to the Rio.

The weather was gorgeous, weather like we rarely see, so we decided to change to Plan B. We will travel all night and aim to reach the Sapodillas Islands in Belize by first light. From there, we will be just a hop, skip and jump away from Guatemala. We will hang out there for a day or two before heading down the Rio.

Plan B went the way of Plan A, when we came across a sailboat, about 20 miles outside of West End. Behind the sailboat was a man driving a dinghy, apparently trying to push the sailboat all the way to West End.

She was dead in the water, he told us, and her sails were destroyed from being caught in the weather from tropical storms Alma and Arthur. We couldn't just leave the poor guy out there like that, so we did a 180 degree turn, and towed him to West End, where we spent the night. We didn't go to shore, but it doesn't really matter. West End is gorgeous, even from the anchorage, and I was delighted to spend one last night there.

"Well, that cost us about $150.00 worth of fuel," said John. "You'd think at the very least he'd invite us over for a beer."

"Oh well," I said. "It might be our turn someday."

The following morning we would follow Plan C – straight from here to the Sapodilla Islands.

June 5

The morning dawned bright, clear, and calm. In order to travel overnight and arrive in the Sapodilla Islands the next morning, we knew that we really shouldn't get away till later in the day. Calm weather like this is a Godsend, however, so we untied from our mooring ball and set off about 7:00 am.

I tried to catch a nap, in preparation for the long night ahead of us, but was awoken by the captain.

"Sorry. I hate to wake you, but you really must come see this," he whispered.

"What?" I moaned, secretly wanting to kill him for waking me up. I don't wake up well.

"They've been following us for about 20 minutes and I knew you'd want to film them," he apologized.

He was right. It was worth getting up to see the enormous school of dolphins – there must have been at least 100 of them. I could hear them squeaking and see them rolling over on to their sides so they could look up at us.

"Ah man, see what we are leaving! Do you really want to trade this for the hot, rainy Rio?" I grumbled.

It was no use. As the day progressed, the seas built, with a huge following sea pushing us towards the Rio, faster and faster all the time. We slowed as much as we could without wallowing in the swell, but we still ended up five miles from our destination by about 2:00 a.m. It was at least three hours before dawn, when we would be able to pass through the reef safely.

So, Plan D was put into effect - to continue on towards Livingston, Guatemala where we would check into the country that very morning. There would be no last minute, three-day blue water reprieve for me. We were Rio bound.

As is often the case when we make overnight passages, Captain John did most of the driving. I lay on the settee up in the fly bridge, where I avoided raising my head as much as possible, for fear of becoming nauseous. I didn't really sleep much, but lay with my eyes closed, so he is convinced that I was sleeping.

While he slept for a couple of hours, I watched the radar and the chart-plotter from my prone position, moving only when I needed to adjust our course. You can't see anything in the black water at night anyway. We were pretty well the only ones out there. During the entire night, I only saw two other boats, miles away in the distance.

Poor John did all the running up and down the fly

bridge for drinks and food, of which I took little, not wanting a full stomach or bladder. I crawled down two or three times to use the head, but other than that I stayed put. I couldn't read or use my laptop without feeling sick. The captain is a salty sort of guy and is able to do anything he normally does while lurching, rolling, tossing and turning about on the open sea.

Sunrise is never quite as welcome as when you are out at sea and I was glad to see our old friend, the sun, back again.

June 6

The captain and I dropped our anchor just offshore from Livingston, close enough to row in. We hailed the port captain on the radio and were told that someone would be out to perform our boat inspection in about 15 minutes. We had cleaned house in anticipation of visitors, showered and changed our clothes so as not to appear like a couple of boat bums after our sleepless night.

A party of six arrived at the boat - four officials who came aboard, including a doctor and a couple of men who ferried them out and waited to take them back. I served drinks as we showed them our paperwork and answered their questions. I thought back to a year ago and how much more Spanish we understand and are able to use this time around, since most of these officials speak no English. The whole process only took about ten minutes and they were off to greet the next vessel, a sailboat that we had passed back at Cabo Tres Puntas.

We were instructed to head to shore to see the port
captain and immigration officer. We headed for Raul
Morales' office. He acted as a boat agent for us,
completing the entire check in procedure while we
strolled around town and stopped for a delicious lunch.

Last year the cost to check in, all-inclusive was $100.00
U.S. This year the price was $135.00, a substantial
increase. We paid the fellow who had lurched for our
rope and offered to watch our dinghy when we came to
shore, and headed back to the boat.

Jim and Jeanie, who were a few days ahead of us, had
planned to stop in Texan Bay, a little spot between the
gorge and *La Golfete*, the large body of water that leads
to *Lago Izabal* and the marina district.

We poked our nose into Texan Bay but there was no
sign of them. We found them down the Rio, back in their
home at Mario's, right next to the slip where we spent
last summer. We had plenty of time for a leisurely tour
of the area, having a peek at the various marinas to see
how full they were.

Hoping to get wireless internet at the far end of the
stretch by Tortugal Marina we cruised by and turned on
my laptop to check for a signal. Receiving no signal, we
turned around and anchored close to Bruno's Marina in
downtown Fronteras.

Without our outboard motor working, we wanted to
start out close to town and research cost and availability
of slips at various marinas in the area. There are so

many choices. It was going to be a daunting task.

It's strange how things turn out sometimes. After all our discussions and planning, we ended up in the exact same spot where we spent the first night in the Rio when we arrived last year.

It was déjà vu, as the wind howled through the anchorage, the skies opened, and torrential rain fell. We were most definitely back in the Rio Dulce!

As I turned off my laptop and crawled into bed beside John, I noticed that the bedding was wet. The hatch had leaked and he was so tired that he didn't even notice it. I could not wake him so I crawled on to a small, dry patch and fell asleep.

He woke a while later, wondering why the bedding was wet and gave me one of those looks when I told him that I had tried to wake him. He crawled out of bed and came back with a screwdriver. Two seconds later, the hatch was tightened and we both fell asleep, too tired to even change the wet bedding. Sleep, precious sleep, with no rocking, pitching, or lurching. It was heavenly.

Towing the sailboat that we found dead in the water off West End

The captain, watching the dolphins as we left West End

Watching the sun set as we head west, towards Guatemala

Watching the sun rise the next morning, as we near Guatemala

329

Our greeting party of Guatemalan officials in Livingston

Limonadas make for happy faces on these Guatemalan officials

Entering the Rio Dulce for the second time - simply stunning!

Who says you can't go back?

Chapter 14

Bruno's Marina

Rio Dulce, Guatemala

June 7, 2007

Who says you can't go back? Not only have we returned to the steamy Rio Dulce, but we are anchored in front of Bruno's Marina, in downtown Fronteras, or Rio Dulce Town.

We are in the exact same spot where we spent our first night last year. It is also the spot we spent our last night, before leaving the Rio in December.

The sights, the sounds, the smells – they welcome me back. The never-ending truck traffic rumbles over the bridge. The chorus of air horns, once annoying, welcomes me back. The deafening sounds of the flocks of black birds in the trees by the stairway leading up to town, from Bruno's parking lot, welcomes me back, as does the overpowering smell of urine in the sun-baked cement stairwell.

Six months has brought progress to Bruno's Marina. We now enjoy wireless access right on the boat. I revel in this new luxury, as we begin to research price and availability of slips in the area.

First, though, we rowed in to Bruno's, the popular downtown marina and site of the most used dinghy dock. We assumed that there would be a waiting list for slips here.

We found Steve and his wife, Monica, the marina managers, in the restaurant. Steve was a gringo, a man of average height, with above average energy. His short brown hair was streaked with a little grey. He wore a mustache and a close-cropped goatee. Behind his oval, wire-rimmed glasses were bright, blue eyes.

His wife, Monica, was from Guatemala. She seemed much quieter than her husband, as she shook our hands, gracing us with a smile that lit up her whole face. Her black hair was shoulder length and the eyes behind her stylish sunglasses were brown. She had perfect, white teeth and a tiny beauty mark just above her top lip.

We have two or three empty slips," said Steve, as he showed us around.

"How much?" asked John.

"We charge $175.00 per month for the slip. Power is extra, at 36 cents per kilowatt hour."

John and I looked at each other. Last year, at Mario's Marina, our slip was $255.00 per month and electricity was 40 cents per kilowatt hour.

Our slip, in the back corner of the marina, had been stiflingly still and hot. We had run the a/c most of the time, at a cost of about $300.00 per month.

As we stood there talking to Steve, the breeze sweeping in from the Rio felt cool and fresh. The first slip he showed us was in a very crowded part of the marina - too crowded for our liking. But the other slip seemed perfect. It was the last one, at the far end of the marina; therefore we would have no boat neighbor on our port side. It was a side-tie slip – even better.

It was the front slip, meaning we would have a boat behind us, but no boat in front of us. I imagined the prevailing wind, coming from the east, washing in through our open hatch. This would mean no need to run our air conditioners, and save us a bundle.

The view of the anchorage and the Rio to the east was equally scenic from both the slip and from Bruno's Restaurant and pool area. We enjoyed many fine meals here last year.

An armed guard walks the docks at night, which is always comforting. John, who has several boat projects on his honey-do list, loves the workshop that Steve showed us. Available for marina guests to use, it is outfitted with a bench press and all kinds of goodies for the captain to use when he takes our outboard motor apart.

Just before we left the Bay Islands, the motor mount bolts, which had taken six weeks to have repaired, broke

again. So, this time, John is going to attempt the repair
himself.

He certainly has his work cut out for him. Besides the
outboard motor, the list of necessary repairs includes
one of our two transmissions, our air-conditioning
system, one of our bilge pumps, and our wash-down
pump. Surely, by the time that is all done, there will be
more. At least our generator is working like a charm
again. Here we will have shore power so we don't need it
but it's great to have it ready for next winter.

So, the decision was unanimous. Bruno's Marina it is.
I'm very happy. It was unsettling for me not knowing
where we'd be for these next six months. I had driven
John crazy all winter, worrying about it. All winter he
had assured me that it would work out, and it has.

We can step off the boat and stroll into town, which is at
our doorstep. We walk down our dock, through the
parking lot, past the workshop and a small but well-
stocked *tienda,* climb the stinky stairs under the tree
full of squawking birds and we are in town. Just like
that.

No more need to make the long, sometimes rough
dinghy ride in to town from Mario's. We can go into
town at night, something we never did last year because
a dinghy ride back in the dark would be unsafe.

Our wrap-around windows in the cabin afford us a view
of all the boats coming into town because they all dock
at Bruno's dinghy dock. We even have cable television
here at Bruno's.

June 14

We are settling into a comfortable pattern of life back on the dock here on the Rio. We are enjoying our new home at Bruno's. John usually wakes up earlier than me in the morning. He tip-toes quietly out of the boat, leaving me the bed to myself, and walks the few steps into town.

No matter how early he goes, the town is up and awake. The litter from the day before is swept into little piles off to the side of the street and burned. *Launchas* come and go to Bruno's dock to our starboard side, and to the public town docks on our port side, dropping people off and picking people up. People are waiting for buses and setting up their little shops and stalls. They are still there if we take a walk at night and sometimes I wonder if they actually ever close up at all.

I like to get up just before 7:30, when our morning radio show on the VHF radio begins. By this time, John has enjoyed a couple of hours with the old geezers in Bruno's Restaurant. He has heard the gossip, read the paper, and drank several cups of coffee. There are several cute, young waitresses setting up for the day, and I imagine he enjoys watching them, too. The local women are exceptionally beautiful.

Over delicious Honduran coffee, we listen to the show. Monday through Saturday morning, a different volunteer hosts the net. First, the host asks for any emergency, medical, or priority traffic.

"Nothing heard," announces the host - after a short silence.

Next up is Mail Call. Any marinas that have received mail for boaters let them know during this part of the show. Also cruisers and sometimes guests of cruisers, who are planning to fly back to the U.S., Canada, or Europe offer to deliver flat, stamped mail to their local post offices upon arrival.

They announce their location, date of departure, and cut-off time for mail to be dropped to their boat. The post office in Fronteras is rarely open and the next closest post office is miles away in the town of Morales. With the high postage costs and slow mail delivery from Guatemala, this is a great service.

The net controller then invites new arrivals to the Rio to identify themselves and those leaving to say good-bye. Next is a segment called Boat-to-Boat Traffic, where people let others know that they want to contact them by radio, after the show.

"*Diamond Lil* would like to talk to *Oasis* after the net on Channel 69," I might say.

"*Oasis*, your phone is going to be ringing," says the net controller.

Treasures from the Bilge is a buy, sell, trade, or give away segment matching up people needing items with those having items available. This is helpful here, where such things are otherwise unavailable.

Non-commercial announcements come next. The wide variety of marina-sponsored events and parties are announced. There are Spanish classes, swap meets (boat parts, not wives), yoga, games of all sorts, special happy hour events, open houses, football parties, July 4th parties, election parties, and movie nights.

You name it - we have it, here on the Rio.

Finally, local restaurants have the opportunity to announce their daily lunch specials and happy hour times. For instance, at Texan Bay Marina it might be chicken-fried steak. At Rosita's, at the foot of the El Relleno side of the bridge, its *hilachas* -shredded beef in a tomato sauce. At Backpackers the special might be egg rolls or vegetarian lasagne. This is a very budget meal, but if we eat there, we usually need another meal when we get back to the boat.

Once the VHF show is over, I check my messages on the computer. I love having internet on the boat again.

John has repaired the transmission shifter and is having the cooler for the transmission welded for $50.00 U.S. He tells me that it will be ready *manana*. Sure, I think.

If that doesn't work, we will have to order the replacement part from the U.S. for $180.00 plus the cost of shipping. We are hoping that our home repair job does the trick.

The bilge pump has been repaired and next on the list is the nasty outboard motor, something the captain hates! In the meantime, Jim and Jeanie, from *Oasis I,* have offered to lend us their four-horsepower motor, so we can get around the river. Knowing how long it can take to get parts down here, we are seriously considering their offer.

There is a never-ending list of restaurants to try in the Rio. Today, we stopped at a *loncheria* that had been highly recommended. It reminded me of the little eateries in Guanaja and Roatan, where there is no menu. They just cook a couple of things each day and you choose from what there is - at a very low cost. We had baked chicken, rice and tortillas and a drink each for 36 *quetzales*, including tip, which is about $4.00 U.S. That was for both of us!

Sometimes, we enjoy a siesta in the heat of the afternoon. I sleep like a baby under the open hatch with the boat rocking in the choppy boat wake.

"How can you stand it?" ask our friends, who stay at quieter marinas.

Yes, there is a lot of wake here from the boat traffic, but I love it. I wake up refreshed as the day is cooling off and have a cup of tea before heading out for my daily walk. John doesn't care for the height of the bridge - the highest in Central America, or the way it shakes when the huge trucks pass by. He's just as happy to stay here and play video games on the computer.

The morning air is still, with the breeze gradually picking up in the afternoon and building until just before dark. By the time I take my walk, around 5:00 pm, the sun is setting and the breeze is refreshing. At the top of the bridge are all kinds of parked vehicles, large and small.

They just stop, wherever they feel like it. I marvel at how relaxed these people are, up on the bridge, enjoying the breeze and the view. They seem quite content to sit in one spot for hours, just talking.

Over the bridge and down the other side, I wander through the little town of El Relleno, which is quiet compared to Fronteras, on our side. Families sit out in front of their houses, talking. Fathers hold babies on their laps. Family dogs lie by their feet.

"*Hola*,"says one friendly person after another. They know me because I walk this way every day.

Upon return to our side of the bridge, rather than taking the steps, down to Bruno's parking lot, I usually continue on, into Fronteras. The little town that repulsed me at first is now my own.

When I return from my walk, we make dinner, making great use of the new barbeque that Suzanne and Russ brought us. The meat choices are amazing here in Guatemala compared to the Bay Islands.

July 4

We are marking the one-month anniversary of our arrival in Guatemala. Also, it is exactly a year ago that we arrived in Guatemala for the first time. We were new to the river then, with much to learn.

We are enjoying our slip at Bruno's Marina. We have ventured over to the *Bahia Discotheque* twice, to enjoy a little night life. The Latin music gets under your skin and it is impossible NOT to dance to it.

Our friends Jim and Jeanie on *Oasis I* lent us their four-horsepower motor until ours is repaired, so we are able to get out on the river. Life on the Rio without a boat just isn't life. I have ventured up the river twice on my own, for my first two Spanish classes. I've moved up to the advanced class and am finding it very stimulating and challenging.

We enjoyed a trip to Morales in a *collectivo*, which is a van that they stuff as many people as possible into. Just when you think they couldn't possibly load any more people in, they stop and cram in a few more. Last year, I swore that I would never make this trip again. This year, I quite enjoy these hot, sweaty, cramped rides. People are so friendly and don't have the same space issues that we grow up with in North America.

Our mission was to try to find two items that we have
not found here in Rio Dulce - a mattress pad and a small
1.5 volt battery for our wall clock. After hours of
wandering in and out of countless *tiendas,* we came up
empty handed on both counts. We had given up and
were browsing through town when I spied a mattress
pad, hanging with some clothing on a line strung from a
pickup truck.

John had noticed a small radiator shop on the bus ride
into town. So, instead of being crammed into the little
collectivo, we walked a couple of kilometers to the shop.
Gabriel, the friendly shop owner thought that he could
repair the transmission cooler that we had brought with
us, so we left it with him.

Conversing face to face, in Spanish, is one thing. The
phone call I placed to Gabriel a couple of days later, to
check on our part, was much more of a challenge. I
understood that the part was repaired, at a cost of
400Q, or $53.69, and that we could pick it up *manana.*

We were thrilled with the price, compared to $180.00
U.S. for a new part plus shipping from New York,
probably another $100.00. Back we went, stuffed into
another *collectivo,* to pick up the transmission cooler,
which John installed yesterday.

About two weeks ago, we noticed a small, six-inch piece
of trim coming loose in our shower. Upon further
inspection, we discovered some water-damaged wood.
John picked and dug and picked and dug. Before long,
the six-inch hole had turned into half a wall.

He was proud of himself when he returned from Mario's
marina with a piece of marine plywood that he had
bought from Frank, who ran the wood shop there. He
cut a piece the size of the wall he had removed. It fit

perfectly. We fiber glassed the edges where the two pieces joined. Now, all we need to do is find a wall covering to replace the one we ripped off.

A friend has offered to pick us up some Formica sheets next time he goes to Guatemala City, the closest place where the material is available. The shower is usable but the job is on hold.

Yesterday, John began assembling a prototype for a new Dorado box unit to allow the breeze to come through our open hatch in the forward cabin but keep the rain out.

We play the "rain dance" continuously. It begins to rain and we close all the hatches and windows. Two minutes later the rain stops so we open them all. Then, two minutes later it rains again. This goes on day and night. Hopefully his new invention will eliminate the need to close the front hatch, which is the main source of breeze through the boat, so we can sleep with it open.

Our neighbor, Dave, has just left the slip beside us. I nicknamed him Super Dave but John calls him Flash. He is 72 years old and has more energy than most people half his age. He darts in and out of his boat and now, just when I have gotten used to him, he is leaving. Now we'll have to get used to a new neighbor.

We're off to the July 4th party at Mario's Marina this afternoon. They are hosting a pig roast and barbeque. There will be horse-shoes and volleyball games. The Sweet River Band will entertain us and there will be an impressive fireworks display.

July 6

Not wanting to drink and drive, the captain and I took advantage of the free *launcha* service to and from

Mario's Marina for the big bash yesterday. We arranged for our ride at 3:00 pm and were picked up promptly, right at our boat.

Rain, earlier in the day, threatened the festivities but it dried up in the afternoon and only rained lightly once we were all under the roof of the Cayuco Club.

The lineup for the buffet seemed to last forever. There was quite a spread; roast pork, barbeque chicken, burgers, hot dogs, potato salad, beans, corn, and even apple pie. Very fitting for July 4th, I thought.

The Sweet River Band had the crowd up dancing in no time. At intermission, we were treated to an impressive fireworks display as the band played first the original and then the Jimi Hendrix version of The Star Spangled Banner.

In typical Rio fashion, the skies opened up, thankfully after the fireworks show but not before our boat ride home. Marco braved the storm and dropped off guests, over 20 of us, at four different marinas.

Unfortunately, our stop was last, after Monkey Bay, Nanawana, and Tortugal Marinas. The pontoon boat was covered, but with Rio rain it doesn't matter. It was driven at us from the side by the wind, under the canopy. Nobody was spared. I felt a chill for the first time since we have been here, as we peeled off our soaking wet clothes and tried to find somewhere dry to hang them. It was the first night, since we've been here, that I didn't need a shower before bed!

July 20

"Tap, tap, tap," I heard on the side of the hull.

"Your banana girl is here," called John. It was all I could do to drag myself from the cool comfort of our guest cabin, where I have been reading for the past couple of hours. It's the coolest part of the boat and one I retreat to when the heat overwhelms me.

Maria, the banana girl, is about ten years old. I met her for the first time last year, at a happy hour get-together at Bruno's.

She showed up, dressed in authentic, hand-woven Guatemalan clothing, clutching a small, red cooler full of chocolate-covered, frozen bananas. She went from one gringo to the next, trying to sell her bananas. I was shocked when most of them shooed her away, or simply ignored her.

Child labor is common here and my heart broke for this sweet child, who should have been in school, not out peddling her wares.

I bought a frozen banana and pulled out my camera to take her picture.

"Fifty Q," she said.

"You want me to pay you to take your picture?" I asked, digging into my pocket for some money, while John shot me a dirty look.

Now, a year later, things have changed. I printed the picture for her on the printer in my boat. Her eyes lit up and I saw her smile, for the first time. Off she ran, clutching her photo in her hand.

A few days later, she was back. This time her hair, normally wound up on her head, was long and had been brushed out. I took her picture, and then chatted with her while I printed her copy.

The child who could barely look at me last year isn't shy any more. She talks my ear off. She has eleven older brothers. She is the youngest child in the family and the only girl. All of her brothers have gone to the U.S., except for a couple who are in jail. She wants to go to the U.S. too. She really wants to learn to speak English.

Sometimes we speak in Spanish and sometimes in English. I worry about her and what the future holds in store for her. I hate to see her out here selling her frozen bananas to the perverts and creeps that prey on helpless young girls here.

Today, Maria has an older woman with her.

"*Mi tia*," says Maria. The woman passes me a large bag of some unrecognizable fruit. Maria looks ready for another photo shoot, as does the aunt. I accept her bag of fruit, knowing that she wants to pay for the photos, in her own small way.

Maria has learned to smile when I take her picture.

"*Sonríe!*" I tell the aunt, but she's having none of it, as I snap a picture of her looking stern and serious.

"Are you going to start taking pictures of all the people in the Rio?" asks John. "The toner is expensive to buy, you know, and hard to find."

"I know, honey. I'm sorry, but how can I say no to them. Last year, they wanted me to pay them to take their picture. Now, I have them showing up trying to pay me."

He isn't impressed. He doesn't care much for fruit. He especially doesn't care for fruit he has never seen before.

July 22

Considering we are living in the rain forest during rainy season it comes as no surprise that we receive plenty of rain! Rarely does a day go by that we don't get rain, and even more rarely a night! The captain's wind - catcher/rain-shield works like a charm and we have only had to close the hatch above our bed twice since he mounted it on the deck.

"Make sure it's removable," I nagged at him. "In case we want to take a boat trip."

The water level is creeping up from all the rain and the daily newspaper is full of stories of flooded roads, destroyed homes and in one case of an entire family that was buried alive in their home when a part of the mountain collapsed on it.

The water is so high that Mario's Marina had the power to the docks cut off. Those poor souls, I think. No a/c, no battery chargers, oh my. Our friends Jim and Jeanie have had to leave and find temporary accommodations at Tortugal Marina. Their generator is not very good and they have engine issues, so don't want to run their engine to charge their batteries.

The water is about a foot from reaching our electrical box, which would mean that our power would be shut off too. So, yesterday morning we did a little generator maintenance, just in case. John tested all three glow plugs in the generator and had to replace one. He also replaced some hose on one of our bilge pumps and tested the new transmission cooler that we had taken to

Morales for repairs a couple of weeks ago. Everything is in order in case we need to pull away from the dock.

We haven't been back to the disco in town. We thought about going on Saturday but decided against it. Good thing because we heard that somebody was shot in the club that night.

"Where do you go to dance?" I asked one of our gringo friends.

"We go to Backpackers," I was told. They have a weekly dance party which sounds a little safer.

August 9

Perched on my bar stool, I am hunched over my laptop in the starboard aft-corner of *Diamond Lil*. One of John's first projects, back when we bought the boat, was to renovate this corner. The built-in icemaker survived the renovation but the rest of the bar was scrapped in favor of a work station. I spend many hours in this spot.

My view from the starboard window in front of me is of Bruno's Marina, the dinghy docks, and Bruno's Restaurant. Boats come and go constantly, giving me plenty to watch. I wear headphones, because the sound of me playing my video clips over and over again, until I get them right, drives John crazy. I slip the headphones off to share my thoughts with him.

"You know - if I had my life to live over again, I would study filmmaking. I just love making these little videos."

347

His answer came in the form of a grunt. He's stretched out on the settee, leaning back against a pillow, quietly turning the pages of his book.

I have just finished making a short video for our friends, Jim and Jeanie. They left Mario's marina for a few weeks and stayed at the Tortugal Marina, where friends of theirs are working as managers.

While they were there, they hired a mechanic to work on the engine of their boat, *Oasis 1.* Jeanie has missed her friends at Mario's and wants to return. The engine work is complete and Captain Jim wants to take a test drive before heading back. They invited us to join them on a short cruise around Lago Izabel this morning. I'm dying to get out on the water, so I jumped at the chance.

I am quite proud of my little video clip. It opens with a shot of the *Castillo San Filipe* in the distance. The Spanish colonial fort was built in 1652, to protect the port of San Antonio de las Bodegas, on the south shore of Lago Izabal, from pirate attacks.

The old stone fort is reflected in mirror-smooth water. The sky is grey with the usual banks of Rio clouds. A lone palm tree rises above the center of the fort. There are a couple of small towers to the left and three more to the right. The shoreline to our port side is covered with low-lying jungle, set against the blue-grey backdrop of the mountains in the distance.

Jeanie strikes a sexy pose against the mast as we pass the low, stone wall surrounding the fort. She wears white cotton shorts and a beige tank top. Her waist length, blonde hair is piled high on her head and tucked up under her white sun visor. She wears sunglasses

with safety straps around her neck. I notice a recent
coat of bright pink nail polish on her long fingernails.

Clearing a triangular channel marker, we pass a water-
taxi, loaded with tourists. I have chosen Rod Stewart's
song "I am Sailing" as the soundtrack for my video. The
words are perfect. Well, almost perfect. We are not quite
sailing. We are motoring, so I pan up towards the sky
for a shot of the mast and furled sails.

I was lucky to catch several flocks of birds, skimming
the surface of the water, and this works well with Rod,
as he sings "I am flying, like a bird, across the sky."

I insert a clip of the puffy, white clouds above our heads,
to the words "I am flying, past those high clouds, to be
free." I suppose he would sue me if he knew what I was
up to. I'm not selling it though, it's just for fun and I'm
sure he won't find out.

I have shots from every angle, so I patch them together
to the long, instrumental break. The lake is like glass,
as I capture the reflection of the clouds, above.

Our inflatable dinghy and Jim and Jeanie's skiff are
tied side by side with long lines from the transom. They
weave slowly from side to side, in unison, in perfect time
to my music. Well, Rod's music.

Ok, so we're not sailing on the sea. It's a lake. And salty
water, it's not, it's fresh water. To the line "Oh, but
Lord, to be near you," I zoom in on John, wearing his
Pete's Pub and Gallery white t-shirt with the black
sharks on front. He, for once, doesn't give me the finger.
I insert a clip of a group of bungee jumpers atop the
ninety-foot bridge that spans the Rio. Under the bridge
we go, under the massive highway in the sky. Past
Bruno's Marina we go, where *Diamond Lil* waits

patiently for us. Past Bird Island, and I zoom in on the flocks of egrets in the trees.

Past Monkey Bay Marina, on my starboard side; past the row of med-moored sailboats, tied in front of matching *palapas*. Past *Sunday's Child*, who lies at anchor just in front of Monkey Bay Marina.

Our friends Dan and Nancy are spending their first night at anchor in their new boat, *Sunday's Child*. They're getting ready to take her out cruising for the first time. Dan is in his dinghy, scrubbing the hull, and he waves to us as we pass by.

Back at Mario's Marina, Jeanie is thrilled to be home. I close with a still, close-up shot of the couple, arm in arm, in the back of their boat. It's a shot that I took at the July 4th party. They're wearing coordinated, his and hers outfits of red, white and blue.

Jim has one of his trademark cotton skull caps tied over his head. This one is navy blue with white stars printed on it. Jeanie's sun visor is white and covered with white sequins. An American flag, also made of sequins, decorates the front of it. She wears red lipstick, to match. Even her star shaped earrings are red, white and blue.

"There. I'm done. Do you want to watch it?" I ask John, interrupting his reading again. He jumps and I realize that with the headphones still on, I was a little loud.

August 10

We've decided that the disco here in town is a tad dangerous for us. There was a rumor that someone was shot there last weekend. We decided last night to try the Saturday night dance party at Backpackers Hotel, instead. It seems a little safer. Our friends tell us there is a good mix of locals and gringos.

As is quite often the case, we sat in the boat, dressed to go out, waiting for a break in the rain to make the trip in our dinghy. As I peered out my boat window, I saw a *launcha* come tearing into the dinghy dock, much faster than one would expect.

We could barely make out forms in the distance, but we saw a couple of men lift someone out of the boat and carry them quickly down the dock, toward the parking lot.

"Well, the rain has stopped. Should we make a run for it?" asked John. He would have been just as happy to stay home and watch a movie, but I had hounded him into going out.

Off we went, in our dinghy, to Backpackers. It wasn't far - just a quick, five-minute ride across the dark river.

"Are you alright?" called a woman, as we pulled the dinghy up to the Backpackers' dock.

"Yeah, we're ok. Why?" I asked.

"There was an attack, just now, on a sailboat. We thought maybe you were running from it."

"No. We just came from Bruno's," I told her. "But we think we saw someone being carried from a *launcha* and along the dock, just before we left."

Nobody seemed to have any facts about what had just happened. The dance party had somehow lost its appeal. John wasn't comfortable watching macho Guatemalan

men strut around the bar with several guns hanging
from their waists.

It wasn't until this morning, over morning coffee, that
John read me the news update from the Rio Dulce
Chisme, an informative online publication.

*"At approximately 10:00 p.m. on Saturday night, four
men with machetes boarded an anchored vessel, with
apparent intent to rob. When they were met with
resistance, it became a cruiser's biggest nightmare.*

*Dan and Nancy Dryden had bought SUNDAY'S CHILD
several months ago, and were looking forward to years
of pleasant sailing experiences. They were anchored off
the small cove near Monkey Bay Marina and Lubi's
house when the incident occurred. Details are still
somewhat sketchy, but in resisting the robbers, Dan
was killed and Nancy, although seriously wounded, was
able to use the VHF radio to summon help.*

*The stations and boaters that still had their radios on at
that hour came to assist, and Nancy was transported to
a private hospital in Morales, reportedly with a
punctured lung.*

*The vessel has been secured, and all officials, including
the U.S. Embassy, are aware of the attack. If anyone
has information that may be pertinent to this incident,
please make contact through the Chisme Vindicator at
photoeditor@riodulcechisme.com. This e-mail address is
being protected from spam bots, you need JavaScript
enabled to view it .*

*The community is mourning Dan's senseless death, and
understandably, is in shock that this could happen to
one of us. Family members are en route from the states,*

and friends here are doing what they can to help Nancy until they arrive.

I was shocked and horrified. Dan and Nancy both attended the Spanish classes at Mario's with me, twice a week. Dan was in my advanced class, a class of only five people.

I had sat at a table with Dan and Nancy after our last Spanish class, chatting at the Cayuco Club. They were asking how we dealt with some of the challenges of living here in the Rio, and specifically about living on a boat.

My last words to them were "If it was easy, everyone would be doing it". It was something I said often, a joke of sorts. Only now, it didn't seem funny. I felt guilty for not taking their concerns more seriously. Who was to know what would happen?

The updates came in over the Rio Dulce Chisme fast and furious. The happy hour crowd was larger and more vocal than usual. It could have been any one of us. There were some tears. There were some people who planned to leave the Rio. Every time I looked at my laptop, there was another update.

Update:

Four men with machetes boarded an anchored vessel Nancy has undergone surgery, and is doing well, expected to have no complications. She stated that she could identify the attackers in a line up.

Rick at Ram Marine has offered to put the boat on the hard at no charge, for as long as she needs.

Update:

The Vice-President of Guatemala, Rafael Espado, has taken a personal interest in this incident. He phoned the hospital today, reported Dr. Rolando, and would like to meet with Nancy Dryden. As he is unable to travel here at this time, after several proposals on how the logistics would be worked out, it was agreed that the family members would be picked up upon arrival in Guatemala City Monday night, and flown to their mother at the hospital in Morales on Tuesday morning.

The Inguat people are invaluable in coordinating, and will be assisting in the movement of Dan's body from the funeral home in Fronteras to join the family for a flight back to the city, where Nancy will enter a private hospital for another day or two. It was important to Nancy for the children to see their dad before he was cremated. Thanks to the Vice President, this will happen. Dan will be cremated, and the family will be here with Nancy for an undisclosed period of time.

We are all sending best wishes to Nancy, who is recovering very well, according to the doctors. She appreciates all that is being done for her and is very grateful to the boaters that assisted, as well as all the Guatemalans who have shown how much they, too, care.

August 15

Update By ROY McNETT, Editor

Local justice -- it´s not a pretty word -- may have been served last night, August 14, when two men were killed in a shooting in the small town of Seja, about five miles from Fronteras and the Rio Dulce.

The two men are believed to have been involved in the robbery and murder August 9 of Daniel Dryden of s/v

354

Sunday´s Child.

Four men were reported involved in the attack on Dryden´s boat. Two of those were reported arrested yesterday, August 14, in the village of Esmeralda and are now in the custody of Guatemalan police.

The remaining two are believed to have been killed last night in the Seja shooting. Their identities have not been made available but several sources of the Rio Dulce Chisme-Vindicator indicate this was a "cleansing" of the Dryden murder.

Two suspects arrested in Esmeralda
The News - Latest News

GUATEMALAN NAVY patrol boat cruises outside of Mango's Marina yesterday, Aug. 14, while police search homes in the nearby village of Esmeralda. Photo by Jane McNett

By ROY McNETT, Editor

Two suspects were arrested Aug. 14 by Guatemalan police in connection with the Aug. 9 brutal slaying of Dan Dryden and the serious injury to his wife, Nancy.

DAN AND NANCY DRYDEN

According to information received from El Periodico in Guatemala City, Carlos Ernesto Lemus Hernandez, 19, and his brother Elfido Concepcion Lemus Hernandez, 33, both of the village of Esmeralda, near Mario's Marina, were taken in custody after a search of their home resulted in the discovery of an ice pick, binoculars believed to have been taken from the Dryden's sailboat, s/v Sunday's Child, as well as a quantity of marijuana.

One source who had seen the body of Dryden said the fatal wounds appeared not to have been caused by a machete, but would be consistent with those inflicted by an ice pick. INGUAT has also confirmed that the wounds were made by an ice pick, not by a machete.

At the time of this writing, seven other houses in Esmeralda are being searched by police, according to sources.

The two suspects were said to be under the protection of a woman nicknamed "Reyna del Sur" (Queen of the South) of Morales, believed involved in various illegal activities in the area, including drugs and stolen outboard motors.

Several local Guatemalan residents confirm that a woman, who with her 14-year-old son, were killed by gunfire last night (Aug. 13) near the Backpackers Hotel gate was indeed nicknamed "Reyna del Sur".

She was reported shot while in the woman's bathroom at Backpacker's. Her son dove for safety beneath the men's bathroom and was shot while hiding there.

August 22

"How old am I turning today?" asked John, in all seriousness.

"Well, honey", I said "What year is it?" That didn't help. He doesn't know what year it is, either.

I once read that for every thousand people who dream of moving aboard a boat and going cruising, only one actually does it. Luckily for me, I married that one-in-a-thousand guy.

We just watched the navy gunboat pull up to shore beside us, here in Fronteras, and load a couple of dirt bikes on board. Every time the ship comes in there are more navy and army personnel on it. The place is crawling with law enforcement types. A series of meetings has been held to discuss the future of security on the Rio.

Yesterday, we survived the intense heat wave by hanging out in Bruno's pool, a first for us. It was literally the only way to keep cool. As I played with the kids in the pool, John pointed out a private bodyguard to me. He was standing off to the side of the pool area, and was well armed. He had his eye on a Guatemalan couple, obviously of some importance, sitting at a table in the restaurant. They were joined by an official looking woman, who was taking notes.

We have seen Nancy several times around Bruno's and have been reading the blog started by her family who are still here in Guatemala with her. They are receiving quite an education about the way that things work, or often "don't work" in Central America and sharing it with all of us.

The Rio is still an amazing little world and the cruising community here is interesting, albeit a little odd. I guess you have to be a little odd to want to live on a boat in a faraway land.

September 9

Time flies and last week Captain John and I met Raul Morales, here in Fronteras, to apply for our boat extension. We also had our passports stamped, which we are required to do after being in the country for 90 days. That marks the half-way point of our six month, hurricane season stay here in Rio Dulce, Guatemala.

Apparently, the tropical storms in the Atlantic have sucked the normal, rainy weather away from our area, leaving hot, but practically rain-free weather. However, I read in yesterday's paper that five states in the south and west of the country were declared to be under an orange rain alert the day before yesterday. Thousands of people are being evacuated from flooded areas.

It is like night and day from the weather last year, which I remember being hot and wet. Today's high is forecast to be 96 degrees Fahrenheit. We have gone local and started using sweat rags. Any small towel or large washcloth will do. You simply wear the rag around your neck or over your shoulder or keep it close by to wipe the constant stream of perspiration from your face and body.

It is also necessary at times to place it on the table in front of you when eating or using the computer. Otherwise, your slippery forearms slide about and make a gross mess.

The best thing to do, I have found, is to try to forget the heat and get busy with something - anything to take your mind off it.

So, while the captain lies inside with two fans pointed in his direction, reading his book, I climb up to the fly bridge and open the windows to let the heat out and get busy cleaning and scrubbing.

If the windows aren't opened regularly, the humid climate grows mold up there, even though the back door area is always open. I wipe and shine the windows and polish the stainless steel. One day last week, we received a beautiful, cool downpour and I put on my bathing suit and went out in the rain and scrubbed the superstructure from top to bottom till *Diamond Lil* sparkled.

John and I climbed the bridge one afternoon after hearing an "attention to the fleet" plea for help on the VHF radio. I woke the captain from his siesta to tell him that men and fire extinguishers were required for a very large fire behind the gas station over at Backpackers. I grabbed my camera and set off at a quick pace up the bridge, not an easy feat in the afternoon heat, to film the fire. John was right behind me. We watched for about an hour, hoping that two large gas tanks would not catch on fire and explode.

I joined a group of cruisers who walk somewhere different each Sunday morning. This week we met at 7:00 am and walked from the bridge in town to the Castillo and then back to Tortugal Marina, a distance of about six kilometers.

We stopped in the little town of San Philipe de Lara at the home of a Canadian couple who lived for many years on their boat and ended up buying property here. They offered cold water all around – to us and to the two dogs we had with us - one which we picked up along the way. They gave us a tour of their home and told us they had family that lived at Roches Point, near Keswick. What a small world, I thought again, as we reminisced about times we had both spent anchored back in our local Canadian hangout.

After three months of trying to find motor mounts for our outboard motor, which are apparently obsolete, John finally gave in and repaired the old, broken mounts himself. Finally, we are mobile and have enjoyed some marvelous dinghy riding. I'm very proud of his resourcefulness - something that seems to be necessary in order to survive in Central America.

With our outboard motor running and our 90 day extension complete, we set off on a short boat ride, along with several other boats from the area, to a lovely little place about 15 kilometers downriver, at the point where the *Golfete* narrows down into the gorge, called Texan Bay.

Diamond Lil, in her new slip at Bruno's Marina

Maria, my banana girl

Removing the heads from the shrimp we bought

John's invention – to keep the rain out but let the breeze in

The ice-cream man, having a snooze at the top of the bridge

El Castillo de San Felipe, Lago Izabal

A shot of *Sunday's Child* – taken just hours before the attack

The Guatemalan Navy patrolling the area, after the Dryden attack

Cleaning the bottom of our dinghy at Bruno's Marina

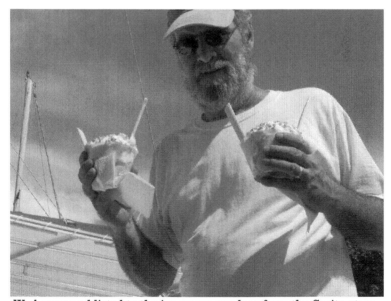

We became addicted to the ice cream sundaes from the Sarita store

My walking companions – Claudie Brachet and Nancy Dryden

Teaching the children to swim in the pool at Bruno's

Maria, my banana girl, posing for a picture with her aunt

Hoofing it across the bridge to buy gasoline for the dinghy

Chapter 15

The River that Swallows Gringos

September 6, 2008

"When you get tired of the big city, come on down for a taste of quiet, country living," chuckled Mike, from Texan Bay Marina. It's an odd name for a marina situated on the Rio Dulce, in Guatemala, thousands of miles from the Lone Star state. Bajia Tejano, the Spanish translation, has a sweeter sound.

I was thrilled to leave the noisy dock and choppy water at Bruno's Marina and cruise to Texan Bay.

The "twins" need to be run every once in a while and it's been over three months. I don't know who was happier - me or *Diamond Lil?* She loves it when we go somewhere and drop our anchor. I can tell. She loves it when I clean and scrub all the places where dirt collects. I can pull on my bikini and clean to my heart's content. We are alone in this quiet anchorage so I can scrub and shine in blissful privacy. When I get hot - about every 15 minutes, I dive into the refreshing water to cool off.

We are in and out of the fresh, cool water. At night, we skinny dip. The water is totally still and the only sounds we hear are birds, jungle creatures, soft, muffled voices coming from the marina, and the odd boat. Early in the morning, young children pass silently by our boat in their *cayucos*, dressed in immaculate uniforms, heading to school.

Texan Bay's unique location makes it a popular stop for cruisers coming and going from Livingston to Fronteras. It's a handy seven miles up the river from Livingston,

where everyone must stop to check in and out of
Guatemala. It's even possible to ride into Livingston
from Texan Bay in the marina *launcha* on the day
before officially checking out - eliminating the need to
stop and drop anchor the day of departure.

When we took the dinghy from our anchorage to the
docks and climbed the hill up to the restaurant/bar, we
were not disappointed. The crowd was fun and included
several people that we already knew. A few were from
Bruno's, a few from Mario's, and several from other
marinas - people we have come to know over the last
two seasons.

The restaurant, which was actually the home of the
previous property owner, Fernando, is perched high on
the hill, overlooking the bay. The seating area for the
restaurant is mostly outside, covered against rain and
sun but open on all sides to catch the breeze. Large,
rustic wooden tables are all pulled together to create a
wonderfully social atmosphere. Newcomers are
welcomed and invited to join the group. This good ole
southern hospitality is what sets Texan Bay apart from
other Rio marinas.

Mike is a large man - not tall, but stocky, with short,
blonde hair and mischievous eyes. His face is dominated
by a large smile, with his teeth spaced just far enough
apart to lend a distinctive appearance. He sports the
bare chested look that is so popular with men in this
steamy climate. His ample girth suggests that there is
some fine Texan cooking happening back in the kitchen.
Beneath the Texan twang is a booming, gravelly voice
that carries quite a distance.

Sherrie, his bride of 30 years, is as petite as Mike is
rotund. She buzzed around the restaurant, never

stopping. No wonder she is so thin, I thought to myself, as I watched her go.

She is of average height, with short, wavy brown hair and an intense, straight-forward demeanor. No more than 100 pounds, she was dressed in a full-length cotton sundress. The twang was evident in her voice also and I sensed a lot of strength beneath the surface of the dainty, feminine character.

When the captain brought up the subject of returning to town, I avoided the question because I didn't want to go back.

"Why can't we just stay here?" I wailed, when he finally pushed the subject. "Look at all these boats. They stay here all the time."

"Come on, Mel. We've discussed this before. It's fun for a few days, but you know we can't stay here forever. We need to plug in to charge our batteries. We're almost out of groceries. And besides, we've paid for the marina for the month. You love our slip, and if we stay away too long, they're liable to give it away."

October 17

The tropical depression that slowly worked its way from Nicaragua to Honduras arrived yesterday, bringing so much rain that the only road to Puerto Barrios has been washed out and in spots the road through Fronteras is under water. The Rio is an ugly brown mess with debris that has been carried down from the surrounding mountains by this deluge of rain. We stayed cozy and dry in our boat and I took advantage of the beautiful, cool weather to bake some pineapple - banana bread. John is wearing track pants for the first time in over a year. It is a nice change from the summer heat and we, like the locals, do not complain about the rain.

As our time here in the Rio starts to come to an end, I am having mixed feelings about leaving. John had a hard time dragging me away from the islands and for the first couple of months I was unhappy here. Now he just rolls his eyes and growls when I mention that I am feeling sad about leaving. We have met so many new friends here and found a wonderful, full social life. They call this the Rio that swallows gringos. I fear that I am being swallowed by this gringo-hungry RIO!

November 4

It's been a busy week here in Guatemala. First, we celebrated Halloween. Then there were back-to-back holidays on Nov 1st and 2nd. Now John and I are watching the U.S. election coverage on TV in the boat.

I was reminded of Halloweens past as John and I poked through used clothing *tiendas* in town, looking for bits and pieces to make our costumes. There are very few toys for sale in town. We couldn't find the toy sword we were looking for, so hubby fashioned his own weapon from a broken fish net handle and what else - duct tape! Have duct tape, will travel!

There was a great turnout at the annual Halloween party at Mario's Marina and the costumes were impressive. There are no costume or party stores or much of anything here so it was amazing to see what people came up with.

The ride home was, as it is so often here in the Rio, WET. We stripped out of our dripping costumes and hung them from every spot we could find inside the boat. What a mess we woke up to the next morning!

Guatemalans celebrate a lot of holidays. We wander into town at night when we hear music and crowds of people singing and watch them celebrating the birthday of one of many saints. November 1st was All Saints Day or *Dia de Todos de los Santos*. The following day was All Souls Day - *Dia de los Muertos* or *Dia de los Disfuntos*. The street was lined with hundreds of flowers and elaborate wreaths, wrapped carefully in plastic, for people to buy to honor the dead.

Millions of Guatemalans flock to the cemeteries, taking flowers and gifts and have lunch around the graves with their deceased relatives. Many feast on a traditional food called *fiambre*. In some towns the skies are full of huge colorful kites, flown as high as possible with the aim of getting closer to the dearly departed, up in heaven.

A new private Naval Police Patrol has arrived on the Rio and is docked at Bruno's dinghy dock next to us. The patrol, funded by donations from key Rio Dulce businesses and INGUAT, the Guatemalan tourism agency, consists of six naval policemen, an officer and a boatswain petty officer.

They can be hailed on channel 16 on the VHF radio or reached at a phone number that we were all given on the cruiser's net this morning. They patrol the area from Mario's Marina to the Castillo San Felipe and with them docked next to us I figure we're in just about the safest spot here in the Rio.

Our weather is cooling down nicely after the scorching hot summer, making life much more pleasant here in the Rio.

November 27

Glancing out, from our anchorage in Texan Bay, I notice yet another boat heading out - leaving the Rio. It's that time of year. Talk everywhere is of departure. Hurricane season is officially over December 1st but for the past few weeks slips have been emptying out and cruisers saying goodbye to their Rio friends.

People seem to hang on the hook for a while before leaving, readjusting to life away from shore. Many of our friends are headed to nearby places like Belize or the Bay Islands. Some are heading back to the States, Others are going south to Panama or down to the Caribbean Islands.

Our current plan is to stay here until after the New Year but boat plans are about as firm as the ground we live on. It's tempting to just pull up the anchor and go. We are still waiting for Raoul to return our nine month extension papers. The joke here is that it takes nine months to get the nine month extension. We'll probably end up picking them up on the way out. It's time to pull out our passports and see how long we have before renewing. That often dictates when we go! In the meantime, we too are on the hook, which brings restrictions and requires more conservation than life on the dock. The phone signal is non-existent, but the internet is good.

We are about to celebrate Thanksgiving - American Thanksgiving. Canadian Thanksgiving is not observed here in the Rio, so I've been craving turkey for a while. Here at Texan Bay, its turkey and HAWG leg! The way Mike announced it on the morning radio net was enough to make us untie from the dock at Bruno's and head on down. I'm thankful to be here.

"First thing I'll do in the morning," Mike told me last night, "I'll cook up some chicken and dumplings. That way I have something to eat while I'm cooking up the main feast."

Mike doesn't look like a guy who likes to go hungry. Texan Bay is supplying the turkey and hawg leg and everyone who plans to attend is bringing a dish or a dessert. The place will be quiet tonight as everyone sleeps off the late afternoon feast. It's a sleepy sort of place at the liveliest of times - the perfect place to wind down from the busy, noisy, dirty life in Fronteras.

Mike drives the Texan Bay *launcha* into Fronteras, 15 miles down the river, twice as week, to stock up on supplies. Any guests who care to ride along may do so, so yesterday John went to town. I spent the morning writing and watching the little swallows that perch on our life lines along the side of the boat, just inches from my window.

I have also enjoyed watching a group of men, who are building a house on stilts out over the water. We watch them every day, rain or shine, working in their bare feet with not much more than machetes and wood from the jungle. Once in a while they fire up a generator to use power tools but mostly it's just hack, hack, whack, whack - amazing what you can build with a machete.

Once John returned from his trip to town, we set off in the dinghy, armed with chart, camera, binoculars and cold drinks - to explore the elusive Rio Chacon Machaca, which winds many miles inland, far into the jungle. We discovered several beautiful rivers and lakes, but the Chacon Machaca was not one of them.

December 4

We joined the exodus of cruising vessels leaving the Rio, on a schedule that quite accidentally copied that of last year's departure. We both felt that we were leaving a different Rio than the one we left a year ago. We took on fuel and provisions and headed back to Texan Bay to wait for the weather window. This morning, we checked the weather sites one last time, and we were off.

We anchored briefly in Livingston, in order to check out with Raoul, our agent, who had all our documents ready from information we had emailed him. He has a kid working for him now, who bikes up the hill to get the passports stamped - streamlining the process even further.

We stopped at a charming little Garifuna restaurant. John had pancakes and I had Thai curry vegetables. By 11:30 am, we had crossed the legendary bar and were out into the Gulf of Honduras. We had not been swallowed by the Rio that swallows gringos.

We had been changed by our experience in the Rio, however. I felt warm and fuzzy, as I glanced back over the article I had written for Living Aboard magazine, about our life here.

All too soon another day has passed and the sun sinks mercifully behind the Sierra de Santa Cruz Mountains, to our west. Dusk is my favourite time of day, when I enjoy a daily walk across the Rio Dulce Bridge, the highest bridge in Central America. The mountains in the distance are silhouetted against a bright pink sky and the mighty Rio runs pink. The road from Fronteras threads as far as I can see through the smoky countryside, itself a patchwork quilt of endless shades of green. The smell of wood smoke brings back happy childhood memories of Canadian cottage country.

As I reach the top of the bridge, my spirits soar and a sense of deep contentment overcomes me. I am not alone in this feeling, as the bridge is busy with others making this daily pilgrimage to glance down at what, to me, should be one of the Seven Wonders of the World.

"Buenas,"or "Hola," - we greet each other, without fail. Gringos and locals - we are one, humbled by the power of the mighty Rio below.

Spanish music drifts across the water and is swallowed up by the racket of hundreds of birds roosting in the trees at the entrance to Bruno's Marina. Pink becomes orange behind the blackening rain forest, its features blending together in the darkening sky. I sense myself being swallowed by this magical place.

Farewell to the Rio that swallows gringos!

Hola Mother Ocean!

We watched this house being built in Texan Bay

Swimming in the rain in Texan Bay

Diamond Lil, anchored in Texan Bay

Texan Bay Marina Restaurant and Bar

Enjoying breakfast with Jim and Jeanie at the Cayuco Club

Mike, from Texan Bay

Texan Bay Marina

The view of the water taxi dock in Fronteras, from the bridge above

Maria

Cheeseburgers in PARADISE

John, looking content at Bruno's Restaurant

Leaving the Rio behind, but not the memories

Birds on the lily pads at Texan Bay Marina

Sherry, trying her new wig on Mike

A dinner outing on the Rio with friends in the Texan Bay *panga*

Farewell to the river that swallows gringos

About the Author

Melanie Wood began her writing career by writing articles for PassageMaker, Living Aboard, Latitudes and Attitudes, and Power Boating Canada. She shared with readers the adventures that she and her husband, Captain John, enjoyed on *Diamond Lil,* their 38 ft. Bayliner Motor Yacht.

A successful six-part series in Power Boating Magazine called The Captain's Log – Diamond Lil Does the Loop left readers longing for more.

In 2011 Melanie published the first book in the Captain's Log series - Diamond Lil Does the Loop, the story of the Woods' trip around America's Great Circle Route.

In 2012 Melanie published the second book in the series – Diamond Lil Does the Bahamas.

Melanie lives with her husband, Captain John, aboard *Diamond Lil* in the historic fishing village of Oak Ridge, Roatan, Islas de Honduras.

She is currently working on the fourth book in the Captain's Log series –

Diamond Lil Does Roatan – Sticky Harbours

Visit Melanie's website at
www.mytripjournal.com/johnandmel

In Memory Of

Since I began writing this book, we have lost four of our dear friends from the island of Roatan.

Mr. Bob, beloved owner of The Hole in the Wall, is sorely missed. John and I had the honor of attending his funeral and I did get to meet his daughter, Melanie.

Miss Yvonne, often the only other woman in the Jonesville group that we hung out with, also passed on, leaving a huge void in our lives. The Hole in the Wall is not the same without Bob and Yvonne.

Miss Kelly, remembered for the Christmas parties she organized each year for the children of Fiddler's and Calabash Bight, was also lost to us. We were honored to be present when her ashes were scattered out on her beloved Caribbean Sea.

Gerald McNab, known by all us as Puky, left his dear wife, Norma, three children and nine grand-children. Norma continues to welcome our gang to McNab place, one of our favorite hang-outs. I was in Canada at the time of his death, but John attended his funeral, along with hundreds of others, islanders and gringos alike.

Dear friends, you are lost, but not forgotten.

Made in the USA
Charleston, SC
19 January 2014